Thomas Frank Bignold

Leviora

Being the rhymes of a successful competitor

Thomas Frank Bignold

Leviora

Being the rhymes of a successful competitor

ISBN/EAN: 9783337261078

Printed in Europe, USA, Canada, Australia, Japan

Cover: Foto ©Thomas Meinert / pixelio.de

More available books at **www.hansebooks.com**

LEVIORA.

LEVIORA;

BEING THE RHYMES OF

A SUCCESSFUL COMPETITOR.

BY

THOMAS FRANK BIGNOLD, B.A.,
*Late Scholar of Caius College, Cambridge;
And of Her Majesty's Bengal Civil Service.*

Calcutta:
THACKER, SPINK AND CO.,
LONDON: W. THACKER & CO.

1888.

To The Honourable

SIR AUGUSTUS RIVERS THOMPSON,
K.C.S.I., C.I.E.,
LIEUTENANT-GOVERNOR OF BENGAL,

WHOSE NAME IS A PROVERB AMONG US FOR HONOUR,
WISDOM, AND KINDNESS TO HIS SUBORDINATES,

THESE RHYMES ARE, BY PERMISSION, MOST RESPECTFULLY
DEDICATED BY HIS OLD SERVANT,

THE WRITER.

LAKENHAM,
    LONG BAY,
        "*Tasmania.*"

CONTENTS.

	PAGE.
The Successful Competition Nos. I to III	1—18
The Rising Man	19
Our Peers	22
The Burglar's Fate	34
Tripos Verses	47
Notes in a Cambridge Lecture Room	52
The Song of the School	54
The Water-Fiend	56
The Bachelors' Picnic	58
The Holiday	65
Song	74
Presence of Mind	75
Wedding-day Verses	76
Ye Stout Mountaineer	77
Old Chittagong	78
Swimming	80
With My Gun	83
A Shipwreck on Shore	84
Tamboobash (Bengali)	85
Adieu	90
The Bagged Jackal	91
Twenty o'clock	92
Acrostic to a Lady	94
Answer to Jeannie	94
To M. Ff.-M., Banyan Lodge	96
A Fanfaronade	96
A Burst of Song	98
Off Venice	101 |//
EPIGRAM—	
In Curolum Dubium Tichbornum	102
Fraus Pia	102
Similia Similibus	102
The Unfortunate Nobleman	103

Contents.

	PAGE
To a Lady with Short Hair	103
Like to Like	103
Actus Curiæ	104
University Scholarships	105
Fancy Dress	105
To my Daughter	105
Lines Written on the back of a Menu Card at Table D'Hote	106
On an Engraving of the Reverend William Knibb, an Anti-Slavery Reformer, Writing	106
On a Station in Lower Bengal	107
The Kilt	107
At the Eden Gardens	107
Local Self-Government	108
Steady Under Fire	108
Promotion by Merit	109
A Matrimonial Notice, "Smith—Armour." Epigram Thereon	109
On a Simla Scandal	109
Trifles	110
Learned Counsel	110
Long Discourses	111
On a Metronome	111
Taking the Cue	111
A Fact	112
Dedicated to the Tent Club	112
Viro Doctissimo J. O. Grant	112
Pool	113
To R. H. Greaves, Esq., B.C.S.	113
The Amateur Printer	114
A Boast	114
Declaration under Act XXV of 1867	114
Prologue to be spoken by Betsy Baker	115
Epilogue to "Dearest Mamma"	116
———— to "Ici on Parle Francais"	119
———— to "Boots at the Swan"	122
Prologue to "The Area Belle"	124
Epilogue to "Bombastes Furioso"	126
CHARADES	130
DECAPITATIONS	134
ENIGMAS	136

	PAGE.
DOUBLE ACROSTICS	137
An Angler's Alphabet	139
An Alphabet of Birds	140
An Alphabet of Beasts	141
JINGLES	142
Question: "Can you Rhyme Sampan?"	144
TRANSLATIONS FROM HORACE AND MARTIAL	146—163
TRANSLATIONS INTO LATIN	164—178
The Artist	164
Ad Pictorem	165
The Night is Still	172
Omnia vincit amor; Quin tu quoque cedis amori	173
The Bellman's Speech	174
Tinnitoris Oratio	175
From "Lycidas"	178
From "The Princess"	178
From The French of Victor Hugo ...	180
TRANSLATIONS FROM THE GERMAN ...	181
Songs of a Wanderer	182
A Heavy Heart	184
Lorelei	185
A Song of Love	186
The Fisher Maiden	187
The Two Chambers	188
Spring Song	189
The Silver Sea	189
Shell Snails and Snail Shells	190
A Wanderer's Night Song ...	191
A Figure...	191
The Rose Bud in the Heather ...	192
A little Song in Praise of Women ...	193
Even Song	194
Slumber Song	195
Song "of Thee"	196
MEMORIES OF THE NURSERY	198
GRAVIORA QUŒDAM	204
Liberty	204
Sonnets on Vexed Questions	205

CORRIGENDUM.

Page 95, Line 14, *for* 'Higieland' *read* 'Hieland' (as in 'Hielander,' p. 107.)

[*It is due to the Author's memory to state that not more than half of these pages have had the benefit of his final revision. Mr. Bignold died in Melbourne while the latter half of his book was still in the Press in Calcutta.*

F. J. R.]

THE SUCCESSFUL COMPETITOR.
No. I.
1863.

"Facit indignatio versum." *Juv. Sat. i.* 65.

OH! for the palmy days, the days of old!
When Writers revelled in barbaric gold;
When each auspicious smile secured a gem
From Merchant's store or Raja's diadem;
When 'neath the pankha frill the Court reclined,
When 'Amlah wrote and Judges only signed;
Or, lordlier still, beneath a virgin space
Inscribed their names and hied them to the chase!

Chained to the desk, the worn Civilian now
Clears his parched throat and wipes his weary brow;
Bound by his oath at every boor's behest
To hear, examine, sift, record, attest,
Recite the whole in dialect uncouth,
And dive in wells of perjury for truth!

Toil as he may, his guerdon is the same—
The scantest praise, the largest meed of blame.
Acquit? And brave the Superintendent's curse?
Convict? To see a dubious Judge reverse?

Commit? An Aryan jury will ignore;
For does not Kali gloat on human gore?
    What tho' Assessors fail to find a flaw,
And trust the Judge alike for facts and law;
Tho' link in link of evidence appear—
Proof piled on proof make clearer and more clear
The prisoner's guilt—the bland High Court shines out
More skilled than Eldon in the art of doubt;
And as the German limner sought to find
Within the hidden chambers of his mind
A Camel—so the Court expects to trace
In past experience every present case;
'Twixt right and wrong an even balance keeps,
The prisoner is released—and Justice weeps.
(Ye powers! I trust the freedom of my pen
Is covered by Exceptions One to Ten.)
    Who shall suffice by instinct or by tact
To thread the mazes of the Squatter's Act,
Enforcing mushroom rights with jealous care,
Yet guarding pauper landlords from despair?
Neglect "demand," and overlook "supply,"
Gaze on pure equity with heavenlit eye,
And without line or plummet, rule or square,
Evolve the only rent precisely "fair."

Who shall suffice his anger to restrain
When daily, hourly, called on to explain :
" Explain why this was entered, that omitted,
" Why A was flogged, and B and C acquitted.
" Since no efficient officer will fail
" In close attention to minute detail,
" Note whence this shameful error of three pai,
" And why Ram Chandra did not dot an 'i';
" Whether he met with punishment condign,
" And, if you fined him, when he paid the fine.
" If not, why not ? Write, in three days at most,
" (This first acknowledged by return of post)
" Whether you think the principle should be
" Applied to all who fail to cross a ' t '.
   " A figured statement carefully prepare
" To show each prisoner's weight and daily fare ;
" Kiss the Jail Code, and certify and swear."
   'Tis not enough in this insatiate age
That pleas and argument our cares engage ;
'Tis not enough the solid hours to waste
Among conflicting precedents and paste ;
'Tis not enough to watch the turning scale
And check each ser of gunny in the Jail ;
To penetrate the city's slums and sinks

Concocting bye-laws subtler than the stinks ;
O'er emigrants an angel-guard to keep,
Harangue them on the dangers of the deep,
Or temper gilded visions of Cachar,
By painting jails and jungles as they are ;
(Alas ! I watch the vanishing Rupee
Worth but one-third the rice it used to be,
And wish that Wood had been as frank with me !)
'Tis not enough—but how shall I pourtray
The legion labours of a single day ?
Is it for this that Granta bade me seek
To mould Ben Jonson in Iambic Greek,
Condense my prose, like Tacitus the terse,
And rival Ovid's elegance in verse ?
Cull roots with Donaldson, weigh words with Trench
Read, write, and talk Italian, German, French ;
Repair to town in pestilent July,
When dogs were rabid, and the Thames half dry,
Abjuring bat and racket, oar and cue,
To spend three weeks disgorging all I knew ?

    Alas ! my Muse, it boots not to complain ;
Who shall restore a service on the wane ?
No longer wooed by fame, or power, or pay,
Isis and Granta proudly turn away.

Ho ! Tinkers, come, and Tailors, share the feast !
I bid you welcome to the gorgeous East !
My die is cast. I can but vent my spleen,
And yield me victim to my fate—Routine.

THE SUCCESSFUL COMPETITOR.
No. II.
1871.

"Hoc agite, O juvenes, circumspicit et stimulat vos
Materiemque sibi ducis intolerantia quærit."

Juv. Sat. vii. 21.

OH palmy days of old ! Oh glorious past !
Long years have circled since I sang thee last ;
Long years of exile on an alien soil,
Where weeks of fever temper months of toil ;
And still I mourn the land, to woes a prey,
Where tape accumulates, and men decay.

(Not mine the Muse Observant* that defames
In disenvowelling illustrious names.
Who steals my style, steals gold ; but he who bends
His parod powers to rob me of my friends

---

* My friend Heeley wrote me, that he had successfully imitated my style in some lines in the "Indian Observer," and that the Secretaries satirised set me down as the culprit. So I took this opportunity of shifting the saddle.

Shall see his subtlest subterfuges fail,
Himself inspected in his safest Jail.)

  I mourn the rule the Magistrate of yore,
A fostering despot o'er his people bore ;
He reigned supreme within his little State,
His smile shed honour, and his frown was fate.
Prompt with the rifle, niggard of the pen,
By manly deeds he won the hearts of men ;
His watchful eye each rival chieftain viewed,
And oftener calmed than curbed the rising feud.
He knew the intense devotion that reveres
Each usage hallowed by a thousand years ;
Nor sought to substitute with ruthless hand
The alien systems of a distant land.
Friend of the people, in their midst he moved,
To all familiar and by all beloved ;
And those who gathered prattling where he came,
Grey-headed now, still gossip of his name.

  Oh honoured Yule ! I would I were like thee,
Dispensing justice 'neath a sheltering tree ;
And, guided less by training than by tact,
Could pounce unerring on the trail of fact ;
For in those days—'tis long ago, my friend,—
Law was the means, and justice was the end ;

Now Rhadamanthus revels in a flaw,
And wreaks injustice while he teaches law.
  Woe to the tyro whose too generous zeal
Betrays a human tendency to feel ;
Forgets to sit in apathy sublime,
And stoops to ferret out and punish crime.
What, if in spite of a parotid gland,
The noblest impulse urge the hasty hand ?
What, if in verity the eager youth
Be seeking, not a victim, but the truth ?
Rebuke awaits his action indiscreet,
And sends him growling from his wonted seat.
  Can the late masters of forensic art
Sigh for the strife in which they bore a part,
Bid Themis bear her lot with equal mind,
Contented still to listen and be blind :
Lest if she once apply the healing salve
Her eyes should open and the bar should starve,
Cursing the bills which brilliant Stephen draws,
Gems of pure logic set in lucid laws ?
I cannot tell ; 'tis not for such as I
To cavil at a Court enthroned on high ;
I can but pray, as Talleyrand before,
That youthful zeal imperil me no more

Thus far I wrote. My ink has hardly dried,
When, true to nature, flows the ebbing tide,
For all things move in cycles; and a man,
A sinewy chieftain from a sinewy clan,
Bids slaves of system leave the fainéant throne,
And learn that fortune waits on force alone.
Up, little Judges! Crime is on the wind!
Fame is in front, and censure lurks behind;
The laziest of the litter-loving host
Must lose his leather, or resign his post;
Then cry, "A horse! my Norton for a horse!"
Mount, seek the curdling gore, the stiffening corse,
Press the pale culprit in his first remorse;
Pounce on the quarry ere the scent be cold!
Strangle the lie before the lie be told!
Then, swift remounting, to your law courts scour—
To smile on suitors at the usual hour.

For the good Magistrate, our Rulers say,
Decides all night, investigates all day;
The crack Collector, man of equal might,
Reports all day, and corresponds all night.
Oh, could I raise my fascinated eyes
From Salt, Stamps, Cesses, Income-Tax, Excise,
Or quit the bench, and loose my courser's rein,

To scour observant o'er the teeming plain,
Could I, with Janus, boast a double face
Incongruous scenes alternately to grace,
To twin tribunals twin delights afford,
Please the High Court, and gratify the Board—
Then all were well ; and I might touch the goal,
A square, round, man within a round, square, hole.

    Then shall I leave the bench ? And duty's track?
Methinks a resolution calls me back,
And I make bold to quote it ; so, here goes—
Forgive me, reader, if it runs like prose.

    " The Court has checked with deep concern
     " A recent quarterly return,
     " And sighs to notice that of late
     " Each chief presiding Magistrate
     " Has let his meaner duties trench
     " Upon the labours of the bench
     " Till darkest crimes and knottiest points
     " Are handled by mere acting Joints.
     " What wonder then if wrong prevails,
     " When striplings hold the trembling scales ;
     " What wonder that convictions show
     " A rate unfavourably low ?
     " For know, the Court prescribes a test

" At once the simplest and the best ;
" And bids its Magisterial staff
" Convict nor more nor less than half.
 " What boots it that the Court enlarge
" The fair proportions of the charge,
" Exception and proviso twine
" Wheel within wheel and line on line,
" Trim, twist, and tinker, prune and polish,
" And then as eagerly demolish,
" If all these pearls of special knowledge
" Be lost on youngsters fresh from college ? "
I must take up some cases : mine the care
To mend the general average, yet be fair ;
For those on High will hardly deign to know
The harmless arts which flourish here below.
Ho ! Minions, bring me fifty chaukidars,
Whose beats deserted to the midnight stars
Cry out for vengeance, and a trifling fine
Shall meet the justice of their case—and mine.
 Thus, having earned a temporary peace,
I turn to count the donkeys and the geese,
The calves and camels that my district yields,
The twice-cropped product of a million fields,
The market-value of exotic grain,

The miles of railway on a roadless plain,
And then, their mythic character confessed,
Try fancy figures by a faulty test,
And prove at last, with philosophic pomp,
How State canals might irrigate a swamp!

 Who cares for calves and camels? Halt, my pen,
The noblest study of mankind is men :
Lay tests and tables on the groaning shelf,
And show how History repeats herself.

 In vain did Joab seek his monarch's side,
In courtly converse deprecate his pride,
Urging the scanty shekels as he spoke,
He might delay, he could not ward the stroke ;
Through the scared land the royal mandate ran
From Tahtim-hodshi even unto Dan.

 Thus, in our days, the captains of the host
Frown on the scheme, and Temple counts the cost.
'Tis all in vain : the bitter blow must fall
On every area-unit of Bengal.

 Meanwhile the peasant in his mud-built shed
Consults his priest, and sways his puzzled head ;
Fears, lest a sacrifice at Kali's shrine,
He lure back traffic to East India's line ;

Fears, lest his daughters prove the Prussian's prize,
His sons wed widows of our slain allies ;
His babies bleed beneath a Bishop's knife,
A plump thank-offering for our Prince's life !
Fore-warned, fore-armed, he takes his sable brood,
Flees from his area-unit to the wood,
Or, wiser still, buys of the hireling scribe
A decad's safety for a modest bribe.

    Or shall I turn to supervise Police,
Bid D forms perish and deception cease ;
A many-sided Superintendent train
To hold a brief, and purify a drain ?
I have no hands ! my only hands, my tools,
One-third are knaves, another third are fools ;
My tools are blunt, or but for evil keen,
And my hands' hands not scrupulously clean.

    Reams could I fill, and yet material find
In the quaint freaks and foibles of my kind ;
Reams could I fill, but wiser I refrain
To rest a lustrum ere I growl again.

THE SUCCESSFUL COMPETITOR.
No. III.
1872 to 1884.

"Difficile est Satiram non scribere." *Juv. Sat. i. 28.*

TO rest a lustrum! I have kept my vow,
'Twere less than human to be silent now;
For topics teem, since George at Belvedere
Thrust a full lustrum into every year;
Himself, and we his panting galley-slaves
Each year a lustrum nearer to our graves.

   Sworn foe to peace, intolerant of rest
His crew despairing and his bark distressed,
His boilers bursting and his timbers strained,
He sought some haven, sought, but never gained.
Wasted in frame, weary and worn in mind
(Bengal ungrateful, India less than kind,)
He heard his leech pronounce it death to stay,
Then bowed to Fate, and sadly moved away.

   Him nimble Dick relieving took his stand,
With foot elastic and prehensile hand,
(For Dick could ride in one revolving moon
On horse, cart, camel, railway, and balloon;

And fearing lest his candidature fail
Could hurry Worcester-ward and beat the Mail,)
" Ho ! knaves," he cried, " I love the breeze abaft,"
And then he eased and stopped, and tacked the craft.

  Yet may we own, our fluttering breath regained,
That not in vain had honest Campbell reigned ;
He found us slow, self-satisfied, serene,
The tape-tied captives of a set routine ;
Then, as a gale beneficently harsh
Drives the dense vapours from a tree-girt marsh,
So Campbell's spirit swept the districts o'er
And left his prefects stronger than before.

  And nimble Dick ? From other lands he came
Resembling sturdy Palmerston—in name ;
A portent he in hero-worship's line,
Himself adorer, prophet, priest, and shrine ;
And who can better an ovation claim
Than he whose proper hands prepare the same ?
For when the Rajas gathered from afar
To meet our Royal Prince in full darbar,
Dick's ready wit dealt promptly with the case ;
His men-at-alms be seated on a dais,
And cried, " Behold these famine heroes shine ;
" If such be these men's glory, think of mine !

" This happy day I feel with graceful pride
" I and your Prince your loyalty divide!"

  Lament, O Muse, the inexorable day
That dawned on Temple's transit to Bombay!
The poet loses what the public gain,
And Satire starves when such as Eden reign.
By nature strong and resolute and cool
He knew the region he was called to rule;
The arts of peace his fostering hand confessed,
The people flourished and the land had rest.
Praise where ye must, be silent where ye can;
Extol the chief, nor cavil at the man.
Him, ere the reins to other hands be cast,
One blaze of triumph greeted where he passed;
And all in one loud chorus joined to tell
How Eden ruled, how justly and how well!

  And Rivers Thompson? able, wise, sincere,
He fears his God and knows no meaner fear;
Loves Honour more than honours; so men say
Who marked him on a memorable day,
Rise from a bed of pain and gird him for the fray.
At Duty's call he came, to combat still
The last pale phantom of a Protean Bill.
I envy not the courtiers who could trace

That gallant heart beneath that ashen face,
On Virtue gaze,* and gazing turn aside
To choose self-interest as a surer guide.
No, nor I praise not those whose anxious eyes
Sought peace in some incongruous compromise ;
Bade will warp wit, and fashioned thence for fear
A screw for lifting conscience out of gear ;
Then aired opinions painfully opined,
And reasoned reasons impotent to blind
Nor least transparent to the reasoner's mind.

    Not such is he who, strong beneath the weight
Of this his all too vast Proconsulate,
Now wields his local sceptre as of yore
He drove the ball and plied the feathering oar ;
When shall he add, ye fatuous powers that are,
The radiance all men miss to India's star ? †

    For they be less than men whose ribald Press
Lives by reviling all that good men bless ;
And let the owner of some honoured name
Go right, go left, defames him all the same.
They taunted him who ailing could endure

---

    * Virtutem videant intabescant que relictâ.—*Pers. iii*, 38.
    † Rejoice, my Muse ! thy line is obsolete ;
      The wrong is righted, and the Star complete.

The Successful Competitor.

With holding, save the mark! a sinecure;
Though he the while was meting out his time
To toils too great for most men in their prime.
O for the grasp of Lytton's mailed hand
To stay the sale of poison through the land;
Nor let sedition sow its deadly seed
And teach the taste that panders to its greed.

    Turn we to Garth, in whom we all admire
The sturdy frankness of a genial Squire;
Since Will now rules where Wisdom reigned of yore
Garth has no seat where Peacock sat before;
Yet holds he brief in common sense's cause
Against the motley group who frame our laws;
And earns the sobriquet conferred in slight—
The 'London Lawyer' pleading for the right!
Nor fails in grave rebuke of their misdeed
Who craving counsel—which they sorely need—
Obtain and cavil, carp and take no heed.

    But what of those who in a loftier place
Would force ambition on a subject race?
Methinks a parable will meet the case.

    A Fairy once with mischievous intent
A new Head Master down to Rugby sent;
A kindly man enough, and one who strove,

As few men strive, to win his scholars' love ;
Alas ! the pity of the thing was this
That all he did was somehow done amiss.
" School for the Schoolboys," ever was his cry ;
(So other men have said, and so say I,
But much—and Gladstone will support me there—
Turns on the meaning that our words may bear.)
He taught—and thereby edified the school—
The right divine of every boy to rule ;
Ordained—for thus would freedom spread the faster—
That every class should meet without a master ;
And, last and best, prospectively ordained
That Senior boys might have the masters CANED.
The boys were jubilant ! But strange to say
The masters all preferred the older way ;
And raised such pother on this trifling cause
The new Head Master could not choose but pause.
Paused, but too late ! The schoolboys from that hour
Were fiercely jealous of the masters' power,
But for whose protest resolutely proffered
The boys had gained the boon so freely offered ;
While anger blazed in all the masters' eyes
Who deemed each boy a master in disguise.
The baffled Head, perceiving how things lay,

Fled from the storm he'd stirred but could not stay,
Bespoke a bishopric, and passed away.

 Ah, well! I like the boys, I always did;
Most boys will swagger—if a Master bid;
Soon as the prime Perturber shall remove
Events will course along the ancient groove.

 Then shall my Muse, in those less troublous times,
In lighter topics deal and Service-rhymes;
Show how the lad who haply made a point
And amber-glued the flies that teased the Joint—
Who, grown a man, at Campbell's keen command
Took gauze-net and collecting-box in hand
And chased statistics fluttering through the land—
Has yet some pins and poison to transfix
The worries of a Judge in '86.

THE RISING MAN, 1873.

(Air—*The Vicar of Bray.*)

When Halliday held merry sway,
 And fiddling was in fashion,
My Stradiuarius I would play,
 For music was my passion;

Nor hushed my string till Grant was king,
   And indigo unquiet ;
Then boldly rushed into the ring,
   The champion of the ryot !
For this is law, that I'll maintain
   As ably as I can, sir,
That whatsoever king shall reign,
   I'll be the rising man, sir,

When Beadon on the masnad sat,
   I shifted my position,
Collecting sheep and oxen fat
   To grace his exhibition ;
And when he broke the amlah's yoke,
   I felt the inspiration,
And learned the brogue of every rogue
   Who filed an application.
      For this is law, &c.

When Beadon's day had passed away
   And Grey assumed his station,
With pen in hand I took my stand
   On—The Higher Education.
But now that lotteries are put down,
   I cut my friends who gamble,

The Rising Man.

And rush my puppy-dogs to drown
 And win a smile from Campbell.
  For this is law, &c.

In framing rules for primary schools,
 In rural exploration,
My active mind shall seek and find
 Congenial occupation.
Then George shall be my king till he
 Shall seek St. Stephen's lobby;
When I shall feel an equal zeal
 For his successor's hobby!
  For this is law, &c.

P.S.—1874.

I hail (since Campbell must depart)
 Our British Bonapartist,
And worship art with all my heart
 Myself a humble artist;
For ever, as my fertile pen
 Some fresh report composes,
I catch awhile my master's style,
 And tint the whole with roses.
  For this is law, &c.

My facile eye can best descry
    That famine's still impending,
And none but Dick through thin and thick
    Can steer us to its ending.
Transactions nice in Burmah rice,
    Colossal cash advances,
Must needs demand the subtle hand
    That guided our finances.
And this I do, and will maintain
    As ably as I can, sir,
For whatsoever king shall reign,
    I'LL be the rising man, sir.

OUR PEERS.
1883.

I.

O Britons, to the rescue!
    For the need is sharp and sore;
The rights our sturdy fathers won
    Shall be our rights no more!
They that be born of cowards
    May court a coward's fate;

But will ye turn to slumber
   With danger at the gate?

II.

No brave victorious army
   Has met us in fair fight;
No stranger of a stouter race
   Makes good the conqueror's right:
The stronghold of our poorest
   Is true trial by his peers;
And our Captain yields the fortress
   We have held six hundred years!

III.

But when the people heard it
   They gathered one and all,
And raised aloft a mighty shout
   That shook the Viceroy's hall:
'Woe to the blinded statesman
   'Who truckles to the base,
'And sets above the nobler
   'The feebler, falser race.

IV.

'Shoulder to shoulder, Britons;
   'Be calm as ye are strong;

Our Peers.

'Come, we will pray our Viceroy :
    " Pause, ere thou do this wrong ;
" Pause, ere thou pluck up lightly
    " The tender plant of peace ;
" Pause, ere thou rouse a spirit
    " Swift-surging, slow to cease !
" Pause, ere the fire shall kindle !
    " Pause, ere the lump shall leaven !
" Hold ! ere thou mock the memories
    " Of eighteen-fifty-seven ! " '

V.

Then, if his eyes be holden,
    And deaf his ears to hear,
Tell him of fair girls slaughtered
    With their mothers struggling near ;
Of judges led to judgment,
    Mock-trialled, hopeless, proud,
With a halter for a sentence
    And the vultures for a shroud.

VI.

Tell him a base-born Indian
    Is the lowest and the least ;

We might brook a Sikh or Sayyid,
    Brave Prince, or learned priest ;
But the school-boy's trip to England
    Is a pitiful veneer ;
And the fear of Brahma better
    Than to hold no God in fear.

VII.

Tell him each man among us
    Would lavish forth his life,
The father for his daughter,
    The husband for his wife,
Ere these pure Christian women
    To glut some menial's grudge,
Stand in the dock, the alien's mock,
    Before an alien judge.

VIII.

Tell him, since Earth was peopled
    And Monarchs have borne sway,
No hand has held so grand a trust
    As that he holds to-day ;
To whom has it been granted
    As unto him this hour,

To will the wealth of millions
  And wield a despot's power?

IX.

What knows he of the present
  Who came but yesterday?
How shall he pledge the future
  Who to-morrow sails away?
Wherefore the chosen statesman
  On whom this charge is cast
Must cease from sunset-visions,
  And scan the pregnant past.

X.

Then tell him how this teeming land
  A thousand years had lain,
Swept by successive warrior-hordes
  And mourning for her slain!
Show how the strong and cruel
  And the weaker skilled to cheat
Became the patchwork people
  That grovels at his feet.

XI.

How, in the ripened fullness
  Of time, at Heaven's behest,

Sailed from a storm-fanned island
 The traders of the West!
Sailed in mere quest of lucre,
 Yet fore-ordained they came,
To break the chains of nations,
 And crown their country's fame!

XII.

Till, as the Indian banyan,
 Sprung of a tiny grain,
Shades with a blessed shelter
 A thousand yards of plain,
Drops from each bough a rootlet,
 A column straight and staunch,
And casts from each fresh column,
 A new and ampler branch;

XIII.

So they, who came for lucre,
 Beneath the hand of God
Stood forth as Kings and judges
 To rule the soil they trod;
Till truth and freedom lightened
 On a false and fettered land;

And the little band of traders
Held Empire in its hand!

XIV.

The fierce Mahratta barons
Before their prowess bowed
The fainéant Kings of Delhi,
The warrior-sons of Oudh;
And each succeeding conquest
Claimed as its chiefest spoil
To free the countless millions
Who tilled their native soil.

XV.

Then as the peaceful triumph
Rolled onward day by day
Crimes that had cried to Heaven
Passed silently away;
No more the Meriah victims
At idol altars bled;
No more the widows clomb the pyres
The living with the dead;

XVI.

The poisoners ceased to poison
And turned to peaceful Art;

The votaries' gore imbrued no more
    The Car of Jagannáth;
No more the hook-strung zealots
    Swung high above the earth;
And if the Rajput dames still slay
    Their baby girls at birth,
It is not that the rulers
    Are callous to the wrong;
This day the babes are counted
    And the curse is not for long.

XVII.

These be the fruits, great Viceroy,
    Of just a hundred years;
These be the men, good Ilbert,
    You offer us for peers;
The hawk in hood and jesses
    Was wild but yesterday,
And can ye loose her skyward,
    Yet lure her off the prey?

XVIII.

Great wrongs, and grandly righted,
    Are there no more to right?

Lies not the land in darkness
　Whose women see no light?
Shall they be sons of freedom
　Whose mothers are not free?
Of blameless truth, whose craven youth
　Was nursed in subtilty?

XIX.

No frank and happy girlhood
　The Indian maiden knows;
A chattel sold ere seven years old
　To a strange lord she goes;
And at an age when English girls
　Are roaming fancy-free,
She sits a dwarfèd woman
　With a baby at her knee.

XX.

But if the wife be widowed—
　The child they call a wife—
Long is the doom and deep the gloom
　That settles on her life;
In penance forced, and fasting,
　She marks each circling moon,

Till the life we saved from Sati
  Is a miserable boon!

XXI.

Pure as the springs of justice
  The sons of Britain stand;
But can they hold their underlings
  From preying on the land?
The prize of every student
  Is a public trust to hold;
And the hope of many a prizeman
  To sell that trust for gold!

XXII.

Shall they be peers of Britons
  Who hold a lie no shame?
Who reckon fraud as fair finesse,
  And only failure blame?
Hire witnesses for copper
  To filch a broad estate,
Or turn the sword of justice
  To stab the man they hate?

XXIII.

These be the wrongs, great Viceroy,
  That thou hast yet to right;

And Britons, only Britons,
  Are with thee in the fight:
Wherefore, since earth was peopled,
  And monarchs have borne sway,
No hand has held so grand a trust
  As thou ——— dost cast away!

XXIV.

The Captains who now serve thee
  Are the bulwarks of thy power;
Chiefs in the van of progress,
  Heroes in danger's hour?
And the planters and the traders
  Are a just and loyal band;
They scatter Britain's garnered gold
  And garrison the land.

XXV.

Shall they be shorn, these Samsons,
  And their spirits not be stirred?
Shall they who count for thousands
  Be units in the herd?
Thou who wouldst maim the Captains
  Who keep the land so well,

Will thy Local Boards hold India
    When their brothers shall rebel?

XXVI.

Thou callest those to govern
    Whose virtue is so cheap
That they tax the poor man's pittance
    To save the rich man's heap:
To govern one another,
    Who are brawling even now,
The followers of the Prophet
    And the champions of the cow!

XXVII.

When,—in the far, dim future—
    Her sons shall cease from guile,
And her Brahmans meet as brothers
    The men they hold so vile:
When her countless castes and races
    Shall have blended one and all,
And British nerve and honour wed
    The softness of Bengal:

XXVIII.

When truth and learning flourish
    Loved for themselves alone;

When, last and best, this darkened land
    Our holy faith shall own :
Then may we share the fortress
    We have held six hundred years,
For India will be Britain,
    And her sons a Briton's peers.

THE BURGLAR'S FATE.

At pulcrum est digito monstrari et dicier " Hic est."—Pers. I, 25.

I.

DUKH Haran Datt was a tough old man
    Though a baniya born was he,
Turning a pice by the sale of rice
    In a small community ;
And all the profit he pocketed off it
    He carefully stowed away
To hold, being old, in silver and gold
    Against a rainy day.

II.

Rings for the nose, rings for the toes,
    Finger rings in sets ;

Collars to deck the swarthy neck,
Chains to be placed around the waist,
Mystical charms to be worn on the arms
    And serve as amulets.
Stored with these were the round rupees
    All in a mighty chest
With a couple of locks and a couple of keys
    Which he wore when he went to rest ;
One is never at ease till one sees one's keys
    By one's nightly pillow pressed.

III.

Dukh Haran Datt had a well-grown son
    Gauri Prasháre by name ;
He thanked his stars he had reared this one
To set him on fire when his course was run,
And travel to Gaya, the land of the sun,
To offer the rich ceremonial bun
    That a father's manes claim ;
A task to be done by each dutiful son
    Who would save his soul from blame ;
For the orthodox view of a good Hindu
    Is that of the early sages ;
That a doom of gloom beyond the tomb

Or rather the pyre, or funeral fire
Is the terrible fate of a sonless sire
  In a limbo dire for ages.

IV.

Father and son one stormy night
Had finished their meal by the flickering light
  Of a rag in a little clay saucer of oil ;
The food they had found so tasty and nice
Was about eight pounds of well cooked rice ;
A dainty our cooks in spite of their books
  Will never learn how to boil.
Horace no doubt would have found some fault
  With the garlic cut in slices ;
But not with the nicely measured salt
Or the spinach and fern stewed to a turn
  Or the handful of savoury spices ;
Forks had not reached that hamlet lonely
And they ate from a leaf with the right hand only.

V.

This to digest they went to rest
  On their mats so neatly spread ;
But they thought it right to put out the light
  Before they went to bed ;

For they knew that Kubér* had no luckier gift
Than a constant habit of careful thrift.
   This being done, father and son
     Went, I repeat, to rest ;
And Gauri Prashád fell a snoring hard
     For the young, alas, sleep best.
But Dukh Haran Datt though his eyes were shut
     His wits were wide awake ;
And he heard a noise like cut, cut, cut,
     The noise that burglars make.

VI.

Now some would take fright at that sound in the night,
     And raise a hue and cry ;
But Dukh Haran Datt did anything but
     And I'll tell you the reason why ;
'Twere a brief relief to frighten a thief
     Who knows one's little store ;
But manage instead to cut off his head
     And he may not come any more.
So gently creeping where Gauri was sleeping
     He laid his hand on his arm,

---

* The Indian god of wealth.

With never a shake to make him awake
    For fear he should give an alarm ;
When he turned in bed the old man said
    In accents mild and low
" I hear a thief! we'll bring him to grief ;
My troublesome cough would frighten him off,
    So you are the man to go."

VII.

His hand he laid on an ancient blade
    That hung on a bamboo peg ;
It was keen and trusty, if somewhat rusty,
    To cut off an arm or leg ;
He fancied he felt the thief in his clutches
And he quoted the words of a fair Grand Duchess :—

VIII.

" Here is the sabre, belabour our neighbour
    " Soon as he burgle his passage through the wall ;
        " Slice off his nut "
    Added Dukh Haran Datt,
" So shall our enemy totter and fall ;
" Slay me this thief to encourage the rest ;
" Sabre his trunk, who would rifle our chest !"

IX.

Now be not unheeding, dear reader, in reading ;
  Raise not your voice in heroic recital ;
I'm sure you'ld be sorry to frighten our quarry ;
  Indeed the importance of caution is vital ;
He is steadily boring away, the sinner,
And the septum of wall grows thinner and thinner.

X.

Our Dukh Haran muttered
All that he uttered.

XI.

As for Gauri Prashád his breath came hard
As he took his stand, sabre in hand ;
  And soon he met with a token ;
He noticed the fall of some clay from the wall ;
It dropped on the ground with a pattering sound ;
And as this was inside he was satisfied
  That the law and the wall were broken ;
" Patience," he thought, " till the hole be larger
" And I'll lay his head like a head in a charger !"

XII.

Heavily weighed the lifted blade
  And he longed in vain for a scimitar ;

But now be it known the hole had grown
    To full four feet in perimeter;
It would seem to some that the crisis had come;
But the thief outside was the pink and pride
    Of his perilous profession;
He had learned, indeed, to proceed at need
    With an excellent discretion;
So he piloted through a thin bamboo
    To explore the landscape's features;
With many a poke to see if he woke
    Any slumbering fellow-creatures!

XIII.

'Twas a kindly night, with a faint dim light,
    And the wind, you remember, blew hard;
So at last he cast his fears to the blast,
Which caught them at once as it hurried past
    And carried them off to lee-ward;
And the deepening shade at length betrayed
That the thief had essayed the breach he had made;
Down with a sweep came the trusty blade
    And vengeance seemed assured.

XIV.

Is it a hit? Never a bit!
It was terribly hard on Gauri Prashád;

For want of a moon he had struck too soon
   And put the thief on his guard.
" Son of a dolt!" the father cried,
" Couldn't you wait till he came inside?"
For indeed the old man was horribly bored
To find such a capital stratagem floored
   By the haste of his hopeful Gauri ;
" As you couldn't cut off this thief with a sword
   " I'll cut you off with a kauri."

XV.

Morning came, and the neighbours all ;
   And Dukh Haran Datt recounted
Deeds by his son gallantly done
   And dangers dire surmounted ;
Nothing he said of his foiled design ;
" My son's discredit," he thought, " is mine. "

* * * * * * * * *

XVI.

Dukh Haran Datt had a little maid ;
Plying the broom was her daily trade ;
   Her cheek had a dainty dimple ;
Her hair hung loose to the wanton wind

And she'd nothing before or beside or behind
    But a figleaf pure and simple.
(Don't be afraid, dear reader of mine,
Don't be afraid of this truthful line,
    For her age was four
    Or a month or two more ;
And the dress that nature gave her
Was as modest perhaps in its plain design
As the low cut dresses of fabric fine
    That at modern courts find favour.)

XVII.

This little maid had a wholesome zeal
That older servants rarely feel ;
    At her task she loved to linger ;
But this morning she ran to her master's side—
" What the dickens is this ? " the maiden cried ;
    " Rám ! it's a human finger ! "

XVIII.

Dukh Haran Datt was deeply moved
    At the singular fact I mention ;
It is hard perhaps to say what it proved
    But the fact defied contention.
" A finger ! " he cried, " what a curious clue !

" It belonged to somebody, Rám knows who ;

" Now—surgical intervention—

" Our Doctor he is a Baniya too, *

" And he knows more physic than ever man knew ;

" Now couldn't he fasten it on where it grew

" With a penn'orth of paste or a ha'p'orth of glue

" Or perhaps by the first intention ?

" For the last I know to human feeling

" Is the most consoling kind of healing."

XIX.

When the word went round that the finger was found

 Back came all the neighbours ;

And a proud old man was Dukh Haran Datt

Of the prodigies done by his only son ;

For he felt that the mouth of cavil was shut

By the very identical finger cut

 In the course of his nightly labours ;

So Dukh Haran Datt though tired and weary

Felt at first uncommonly cheery.

XX.

Now the purest pleasure on earth, my brother,

Is winning a hand that belongs to another,

 The soft warm hand of one's dearie :

---

 * He was, and a Surgeon-Major in the Army.

But winning a finger that isn't our own
Is a feeling perhaps we have few of us known,
And if that finger be cold as a stone
It's trying indeed to one's nervous tone ;
   Dukh Haran found it eerie ;
So hurrying off to the nearest station
He laid a criminal information
With the finger to warrant the whole narration ;
   But the name of the thief was—Query ?

   *   *   *   *   *   *   *

XXI.

Pegasus, tack ; carry us back
To follow the thief on his lonely track.

XXII.

The blow had fallen, the robber arose,
   He slipped through the hole and out of the street ;
He hurried away from his baffled foes
   But his hand seemed terribly incomplete.

XXIII.

Had he lain concealed till the finger was healed
   He had met no further question ;
For his hut was distant many a mile ;

But he parleyed awhile with the Spirit of Guile
    Who offered this suggestion :
" Weave a pretence for a false defence ;
    " They'll spot you, I shouldn't wonder."
So away went he to Darogha-Ji
    With the wound he laboured under
And reported a fight with thieves at night
    Who had cleft his hand asunder !

XXIV.

The Darogha knew this couldn't be true ;
    He had nothing to steal, poor knave ;
And the peeler knew how the adage ran,
For a poet has said that a penniless man
May travel unarmed, and sing, if he can,
    At the mouth of a robber's cave ;
(So Victor Hugo's nervous coves
In the shade of the trembling aspen-groves
    Found comfort in a stave.)
The Darogha cried " I'll wager a crore
" We shall have a complaint ere the day be o'er
    " He has been in a drunken brawl ;"
But the officer wondered more and more
    For there came no charge at all ;

So wondering much what the man's deceit meant
He sent him in for medical treatment.

* * * * *

XXV.

Down in the town sat Major Brown
    Hearing Police reports ;
His daily fate between six and eight
    Ere the sitting of the Courts ;
But never as yet had he happened to get
    As he sat at his early desk
Two informations from different stations
    That read so like burlesque ;
A fingerless thief at Pár Kalinga
And at Dukh Haranpur a thiefless finger !

XXVI.

The thief, as it proved, was a man who had moved
    At the head of his profession ;
He was sent (the Joint decided the point)
    And tried by the Court of Session ;
He hadn't the face to frame a case,
    Confessed, and was convicted ;
And the sentence—well, 'twas no end of a cell
    And liberty long restricted.

P. S.

My medical friends may wish to know
  If the finger reunited :
The surgeon was clever as surgeons go
And I really think it would have been so
  But his hopes were oddly blighted ;
He was eagerly pacing to and fro
While the finger was warmed in a basin below
When down swooped something, a kite or a crow,
And carried it off en haut, en haut,
  And the de'il knows where it alighted !

TRIPOS VERSES.

1857.

THERE is a time-honoured custom at Cambridge, which ordains that, on the reverse of the Honour Lists, should be printed, at the cost of the University, some satirical verses furnished by under-graduates, who have, for the nonce, the utmost liberty of caricaturing their elders. The following is a specimen. The plays upon the names of Proctors and pro-Proctors, Day, Wolff, Lamb, and Provost Okes explain themselves. Eunicus is of course no other than the kindly and popular Harvey Goodwin, and Creticus is Chalker the Proctor, who was the natural enemy of under-graduates, and who, the better to stalk them, was said to hide his bands. Κρῆτες ἀεὶ ψεύσται κακὰ θηρία. Σ and K are Shilleto and Kennedy.

Fescennina per hunc inventa licentia morem.—*Hor. Ep.* 2, 1, 145.

QUÆREBAM nuper notæ qui prata Cotonæ
Calcaret mecum ; mihi mox occurrit amicus
Nec mora, namque ultro comitem se præstat eunti.

Optimus ille quidem, nec qualis triste suile
Incolit, atque horas viginti quinque laborat;
Noster enim Etonæ spiraverat æthera purum
Otia prætextâ meritus peragenda togato.
Cura tamen comitis non sueta in fronte sedebat;
Cui nos: Qui tantus dolor, o Regalis alumne?
Tene foris vidit tabulâque togâque carentem
(Proh nova monstra) Dies noctu? vel Creticus iste
Creticus obductâ celans insignia palmâ?
Vel qui vestimenta Lupi nunc induit Agnus?
Rura times? Venerisne puer te ludit amantem?

Parce rogare, comes; non sunt mihi talia curæ!
Nec me ludit amor, nec sacra nocet mihi sindon
Granta ruit; periitque pudor, periitque vetusta
Justitia et pietas; urnas jactamus avorum.
Magna fuit quondam cineris reverentia cari,
Inque suo pretio qui munera codice largo
Magna daret Grantæ; nunc insultare sepulchro
Mos est, et fatui contemnere jussa datoris.
Mox, nisi desuetam renovârint bella coronam
Intermissa diu, forsan novus incola nobis
Dixerit: Hæc mea sunt; veteres migretis alumni.
Regales saltus cuivis habitare licebit,
Custodisque loci Quercûs requiescere in umbra.

Narras, concedo, durissima ; nec tibi suave est
In veterum libris longos consumere soles ;
At ne te fortunam et iniquæ tædia sortis
Oppressisse putes solum, da, si vacat, aurem.
Vita hominis vapor est, et amaro plena dolore ;
Vix semel exultare datur ; mox occidit, eheu !
Occidit ; irato franguntur numine nares.

    Nestor erat princeps, nullo comitatus ; at ille
Qui tot sustinuit, qui tanta negotia solus
Interiit ; Gallo ferus insidiabitur exsul ;
Δηρόβιοςque brevi mentito nomine regnat.

    Cælicola en princeps, cui frater Delius, et cui
Luna soror, nostri stupet ignea fulmina Martis ;
Iratum* et sentit Cantonæ fictile Taurum.
Tunc dolere potes, tua sors tibi dura videtur
Quum grave perfidiâ, missumque recenter ab Indis
Τηλεγράφημα legis ? (non quod tu scribis inane,
Bospore ; nec Tripodum verbum est aptare Camœnis.)
O utinam quæ nunc insanit lege soluta
Arbitrio legis† rursus colat India pacem.
Stat moribunda manus mercatorum, gravis annis,

---

* Βοῦς ἐν πόλει· sc., ἐν τῷ Κεραμεικῷ. (Schol.)
    Minime respicit hic locus id quod de Hibernis Æschylus " Βοῦς ἐπὶ γλώσσῃ μέγας."

† Vide Burkii Album Nobilium, s. v. Ellenborough.

Quae nigros terret, tristis venerandaque Morino,
Incertos uno capite, an sit praedita centum.
Tabet Honoratum nomen ; fugere sagaces
Mures ; insolito tremuit vicinia motu
Atque Aula impendens expectat Plumbea lapsum.

    Ad Grantam redeo : hic sua quemque molestia rodit ;
Volvitur illi alter, volat huic jam tertius annus ;
Ille Proexetasin timet ; hunc Ingentia terrent.

    Annum praeteritum memini, miserabile tempus ;
Vix ipse effugi ; tantum potuere soporis
Gaudia, et hesternus labor ; at suavissimus unus
Nostras defendit partes Eunicus, et iram
Inquisitorum vicit ; sic alite faustâ
Servavi horrentes mirâ dulcedine pennas.

    Sunt quibus ipse suis unâ Sol luce labores
Distulit ; o nimium infaustos, si nubila densas
Tempora pressissent duplici caligine mentes.

    Interea Grantâ egreditur venerabilis ordo
Qualibus ille Faber largitur praemia divus ;
Qua via ferrea se longe deflectit ab urbe.
Omnibus hanc opus ire viam ; speculumque tubasque
Devehit astronomus ; fulget Sol luce secundâ.
Mox itur tarde maestae per stagna paludis ;
(Hos latices non est operae cognoscere, cives.)

Vix ventum est ad fana Petri ; et nigrantibus, eheu !
Obscurus subito densatur nubibus æther.
Baileji globulos cupimus discernere ; frustra ;
Vidimus hoc solum miseri, nil posse videri ;
Et vitrea in triviis reduces projecimus arma.
(Sic olim, si fas magnis componere parva
Attica tot naves Siculas emisit in undas ;
Sic fractæ periêre rates, ægræque catervæ.)
   Nos ædes colimus tenui tibicine fultas
Magnâ parte sui, nam sic labentibus obstat
Villicus, et veteris rimæ quum texit hiatum,
Securum pendente jubet dormire ruinâ.
Heu ! mihi vivendum est ubi multa* incendia, multus
Nocte metus. Quis enim non dira incendia, lapsus
Tectorum assiduos, urbisque pericula vitet
Mille, et Quinctili recitantes mense poetas.
Hic, si certamen sibi proposuêre canorum,
Qui studet optatam versu contingere metam
Conquirit, (qualis vel nos vel mitis Eastes)
Quid Sophocles et Flaccus et Æschylus utile narrent.
Sic læti pueris tradenda numismata condunt.
At cave concessum nimium veteres imitandi

---

* Hoc satis intellexerint qui benevolentiâ singulari totam horam noctu aquâ afferendâ consumpserint.

Jus credas ; si liberius quid scripserit auctor
Huic ultro properant nigrum præponere Theta
Exemplumque negant, gestandis quotquot alumnis
Optatam ad metam meriti sint nomina " Currus."
Ergo age, nec veteres auctores volvere cura ;
Sed captare leves Camensis Arundinis auras,
Vel quam nexerunt nullâ non arte Corollam
Clarum Sabrinæ genus, et cum Sigmate Kappa.

Talibus exemplis veterem solabar amicum,
Jamque parallelas (qua remex turba laborat)
Cœpimus ire vias ; resonat campana sacelli,
Et vacuum revocat quod servat janitor album ;
Ergo ille ad Regis properat discedere turres ;
Ipse ego labentes pedibus pulsare tabernas.

NOTES IN A CAMBRIDGE LECTURE ROOM.

Will you come to the lecture to Day ;
   For then you'll undoubtedly find
That if you 've a mind for a rest
   He'll give you a rest for your mind.

A basket comes leading the way,
   A score theologians within ;
And ten minutes later comes Day
   With volumes piled up to his chin.

Notes in a Cambridge Lecture Room.

His lecture diluted arrives ;
    Each paragraph calls for a search ;
And while to compile it he strives,
    His hearers are left in the lurch.

Some trifle he doubtfully says ;
    Then passes his hand through his hair ;
And next for some minutes surveys
    His boots with a gratified air.

At chapel sometimes he appears,
    But 'dearly beloved' eschews ;
Poor French, when the signal he hears,
    May frown, but he dare not refuse.

At once to the portal he hies
    Day's sesame opens the locks ;
We soon see the curtain arise
    And Day follows close on his knocks.

But truce to these playful assaults ;
    Be quiet, my muse, if you can ;
I would not be hard on the faults
    Of
        A Norfolk Classical Man.

THE SONG OF THE SCHOOL.

Written by command of a bevy of fair girls at Oakwood, Simla, 1878.

I.

Rise, rise, rise,
   When the morning light is grey,
Fresher than flowers
In the early hours
   For another busy day.

Down, down, down,
   To the schoolroom desk and book;
In the care and strife
Of the afterlife
   You may long for this mountain nook.

   Work, work, work,
      'Neath a wise and kindly rule;
   Busy at work, and merry at play,
      Singing the Song of the School.

II.

Work, work, work,
   Through the solid hours of day,
You 'll wonder how soon
'Twill be striking noon ;
   Then merrily off to play.

Race, race, race,
   Through the air so crisp and cool ;
Join in a chase
With girlish grace
   Singing the Song of the School.

   Then work, work, work,
      'Neath a wise and kindly rule ;
   Busy at work, and merry at play,
      Singing the Song of the School.

III.

Work, work, work,
   When the hours of day are past ;
Till the candles are burnt
And the lessons are learnt
   And bedtime comes at last.

Wink, blink, wink,

  Till Henry the Eighth, and France,

And the Rule-of-Three,

And the Caspian Sea

  Join hands in a medley dance;

  Then bed, bed, bed,

    In your rooms so clean and cool;

And wake up bright with the morning light,

  Singing the Song of the School.

THE WATER-FIEND.

There is a very fine reservoir at Gaya named Bisárh, near which no native will venture after dusk, as it is said to be haunted by a *Bhút*, or devil.

Pandúbi is one who dives himself. Pandubáli is one who is the cause of diving in others.

  Said Ganga Bishn to Rádha Krishn:

    "Come along fishin', it is not far;

    "I'll bet you a kauri, the evening's showery

      "And the fish bite freely in broad Bisárh."

  Said Rádha Krishn to Ganga Bishn:

    "Your heart is wishin' the same as mine;

    "I've forgotten the look of a Limerick hook

      "And this is the weather to wet a line."

"But," said Rádha Krishn, "on one condition;
    "We mustn't get caught by the evening star;
"For a diving devil is known to revel
    "Below the level of broad Bisárh."

They have chosen their nooks, and baited their hooks,
    And the fish bite freely in broad Bisárh;
Intent on their curry, they do not hurry,
    When stealthily peeps the evening star!

"O Rádha Krishn," cried Ganga Bishn,
    As out went a thousand yards of sút,
"As sure as fate he has gorged my bait
    And I've hooked the Pandubáliyá Bhút."

"O Rádha Krishn, dear Rádha Krishn,
    "Lend me a helping hand, I beg!
"For the bank is steep, and the tank is deep
    "And the line is twisted round my leg!"

Said Rádha Krishn, "With your permission,
    "I'd rather not stay 'neath the evening star;"
So he fled from the bank, and his poor friend sank,
    And the *Bhút* had dinner in broad Bisárh.

THE BACHELORS' PICNIC.

A Lay of Modern Coonoor.
1868.

I.

Ho, Ladies! twine your pagris
   And don your habits all;
The Bachelors invite you
   To Law's famed waterfall.
The Bachelors invite you
   To grace their feast to-day,
And Charlie Gray, no churlish host,
The fatlings of his flock shall roast—
   And Honeywell, they say,
Shall send the best his cellars boast,
That sparkling jest and loyal toast
   May wile the hours away.

II.

Now many a swarthy coolie
   Beneath his burden bends;
Far down the rugged road-way
   The dusky line extends;
And horses now, and ponies
   Champ at each lady's gate;

Right eager are those gallant steeds

    To bear so fair a freight!

III.

Green are the groves whose gum-trees

    Our steep hillsides adorn ;

Fair are the ferns whose frondage bends

    Beneath the dews of morn ;

The Reading-room is furnished

    With dusty tomes and dull ;

Best of all hills the Sámbar loves

    The Drúg of Húlikal.

IV.

But now beneath the gum-trees

    No morning caller strays ;

No florist culls the dewy fronds

    That deck the winding ways.

High on the Drúg the Sámbar

    Graze fearless of the ball ;

The dusty tomes unheeded lie

    Along the dusty wall.

V.

For lo! the clouds have lifted,

    The rain has passed away,

The very skies are smiling
  On this our Picnic day.
Shame on the lad who loiters
  When love and beauty call ;
Coonoor has sent her fairest forth
  To Law's famed waterfall.

VI.

And now we reach the valley
  Within whose deep ravine
'Mid foam and mist, and glittering spray
  The waterfall is seen.
Right deftly tread the ladies
  Along the perilous rock,
For each has grasped a stalwart hand
  And needs no Alpenstock.

VII.

While on the view before us
  Our eager eyes are cast,
The 'boys' unfold a snowy cloth,
  And range the choice repast.
Soon knives and forks are busy ;
  No sinecure have they
Who brew the sparkling claret cup
  On this our Picnic day !

VIII.

But when the liquid jelly
    Had marked the banquet's close,
Then all to cross the torrent
    With one consent arose.
The knights mid shouts of laughter,
    And screams, and feigned alarms,
They bore across the ladies
    All cradled in their arms!

IX.

Lo! who is this that taketh*
    His pastime in the deep?
What lithe amphibious monster scales
    Each slimy, slippery steep,
Or lurks in gloomy caverns
    Where sun-light may not gleam?
Those limp and dripping garments mark
    The genius of the stream!

---

* Captain V. Law, the discoverer of this beautiful waterfall, and engineer in charge of the hill road; as good a swimmer as he was a guide. I shall not forget his showing me the beauties of the place on an earlier occasion, and his endeavour to get me across the stream. He could jump from one pointed boulder to the other over the torrent. I couldn't. So he cut a sapling; and as he was settling one end on his point of vantage, and I was supporting the other, he dislocated his shoulder, and brought down the sapling on my finger, crushing it. The pain we each endured was considerable; but the situation—each of us perched on a pointed stone, and writhing at one another across the stream was so exquisitely ridiculous that we laughed loudly. He put his shoulder in again, and we went on.

X.

But see! a pale Bengali*
　With plate excited, stands;
His spider-spindled engine
　Is planted on the sands;
And as he waves the signal,
　Behold on one and all
Where late was life and laughter,
　A sudden stillness fall.

XI.

At last the weary seconds
　Have ticked their length away;
The ladies turn to prattle
　As school-boys to their play.
The picture once developed,
　The pale Bengali locks
His spider-spindled engine
　Deep in his brass-bound box.

XII.

But when the sun was sinking
　Behind the western ridge,
We left the happy valley
　And gathered on the bridge;

---
* Myself.

Then with a GRACE to guide us
  In nature as in name,
We played before we parted
  A good old English game.

XIII.

And then we cried the forfeits,
  As merry folk should do;
And MUCH* we saw to laugh at
  And MUCH to envy too;
For on the sad Knight-errant
  A maiden laid command,
To wait on every lady
  And kiss her lily hand.

XIV.

And as he ran the gauntlet
  'Twas something to admire,
The way he turned his rosy lips
  Toward his trusty Squire.
And ever as he turned, the Squire,
  With light and airy grace,
Wiped on a tattered handkerchief
  The sad Knight-errant's face!

* The name of a gallant Lieutenant.

XV.

But now the day was closing,
 As brightest days must close;
And all the knights and ladies
 With one consent arose.
The gallant steeds were ready,
 And lightly every lass
Was lifted to her saddle
 And hied her up the pass.

XVI.

And oft, amid the labour
 Which waits us in the Plains,
Parched by the heats of April,
 Or drenched by August rains,
By many a league tho' severed,
 'Twill please us to recall
The Picnic of the Bachelors
 At Law's famed waterfall.

———

THE HOLIDAY.

Port Blair.

Indian readers, after perusing the following veracious chronicle, may be disposed to prefer the trip in question to many others which may be accomplished within the limits of a month's or even of three weeks' privilege leave. Those who do so will find on board an excellent table, plenty of ice, and the utmost possible care for their comfort and for their enjoyment too. It is only to be added that the number of steamer cabins is not great, so that readers cannot all go at once.

EMBALM, O Muse, in an appropriate lay
  The worn Civilian's well-earned holiday;
Touch lightly on the hours of weary pain
And wasting sickness combated in vain;
Tell how the leech exhausted all his store,
Tell how the sufferer murmured "Hold! No more!"
Till wife and leech and patient did agree
To trust Dame Nature and a trip to sea.

  A trip to sea! but whither, gentle Muse?
The waves are all before us, where to choose;
Bound for what port, of all the ports that are?
Ceylon is muggy, and Hongkong too far;

So let me rather, whose judicial care
Has quartered many a convict on Port Blair,
Sign my own warrant with my own consent
Affirming thus my proper precedent.

    Next to arrange the details of my plan ;
Shall I set sail, a solitary man—
I, round whose neck some seventy fingers twine
The pleasant tendrils of the clustered vine ?—
No ! 'tis not good for man to live alone,
And Adam needed Eve, and Darby Joan ;
And I with wife and children will embark
A band two short of Noah's in the ark.
So said so done ; selecting as our scene
The eastern alias of our gracious Queen,*
Anon to Hastings jetty we repair,
Cast by kind Fate on kindly Burleigh's care.

    Him had his sire with clear prophetic view
Named from the God of sinew and of thew
Who, in the early days when Earth was young,
Strangled the snakes that on his cradle hung.
His waxing might be plighted to the seas,
And here he stands—a burly Hercules.

    How fair are strength and beauty when allies !

---

* S. S. "Maharani."

Love in her smile, and laughter in her eyes,
For Burleigh is her idol, who but he?
His fair fond Florence sails in company;
Nor only she; their cabin is the home
Of two wee fairies, daughters of the foam.

    A son of Mars, whose skilful pen pourtrays
All that his just theodolite surveys——
A man of peace, who plucks from India's field
A leaf more fragrant than Cathay may yield—
These are our party, well equipped and found
In pluck and all good humour for the round.

    We found strange weather as the dying day
Saw Ganges broaden on the treacherous bay;
The clouds hung low and broken, and the deep
Seemed slowly waking from a troubled sleep;
Boreas, whose breath had fanned us through the day
Light as the touch of tiger-whelp at play,
Was now the tiger as he hurled forth
The ruthless champion of the rugged North.

    The mystic casket fraught with conscious void,
Brass frame of quivering nerve, the aneroid,
Felt the light load and indraught near at hand,
Inferred the storm, and, tender of our band,
Through many a lever drooped a warning hand.

Our Captain saw the omens, nor in vain;
Knew the dread cyclone of the Southern main;
Huge twirling Top, launched by no mortal power,
Weird Whirlwind-dial's retrograding hour;
Invoked the blast 'twas madness to defy,
Swerved to the South, and let the doom pass by.

Joy to the lads whose breath came glad and free
Amid the lurches on that rolling sea;
Woe to the ladies in their cabins pent
Who could not brook the labouring element;
Till calmer seas bespoke the milder air,
And halcyon weather sped us to Port Blair.

O favoured isles of Heaven! O lovely scene!
Whose wooded heights slope down to seas as green,
Save where the wave, dashed on some reef below,
Lights the long base with clouds of wreathed snow.
Here, Mercy tempering Justice, for a time
Britannia gathers India's sons of crime.
Not theirs to pine in dungeons or in chains,
Chilled in the cold, or mouldering in the rains;
Here must they toil, but free, or all but free,
Their only prison-wall the girdling sea!
Toil, but in hope; for wisdom bids them learn
The sweets of honest effort, and to earn

The stipend of their labour, until time
Fill the full tale of years that expiates their crime.

    Aye, all may hope! for even he whose knife
Has dealt a death-blow to another's life,
He whose own life were forfeit, knows that he
When twenty years have rolled, shall yet be free;
Seek the dear village where a boy he played,
The little temple and the banyan-shade,
Rejoin his children grown to man's estate
And early friends still mourning for his fate;
Pluck the rich harvest of the mangoe groves,
And breathe his last among the scenes he loves.

    O brothers of the ermine, who in Ind
Award their fate to thousands who have sinned,
Deem not that doom vindictive or severe
Which saves a wretch from Jail, and sends him here!
But grant henceforth (what thoughtful Judge would not?)
The more deterrent but the milder lot.

    Here convicts clear the jungle, plant the tea;
Yon coral pier that breaks the angry sea
Was piled by convict hands; the cargo boats,
This busy fleet that round our steamer floats,
Were built, are manned by convicts; convict toil
Your linen laves, and fills your lamp with oil.

Turn we from crimes and convicts, Muse, awhile,
And hymn the social honours of the isle.

Soon as the anchor thunders to its bed
A swift boat glances from the jetty-head;
Twelve sturdy rowers of Panjabi race
Bend to the oar and urge the speed apace.
No prisoners they; since Mayo, good and great,
Fell less by convict than fanatic hate,
These towering Sikhs, broad-chested, iron-hard
Ply the Chief's oars, and form his body-guard.
And none need ask a doughtier following
Than this, the gallant band of Teja Singh.

These, from his seat of Government on Ross
Speed the Chief near us; whom Victoria's Cross
Adorns, for deeds of mark in days gone by,
When India travailed in the Mutiny.

The boat alongside, prompt the Chief appears,
Not fifty yet, and younger than his years;
If any doubt, lawn-tennis be my witness
Of youth and pluck and energy and fitness.

What is his errand as he mounts our deck?
—To place his gig, launch, escort at our beck;
And, last and best, fair welcome to afford
To his most choice and hospitable board.

The Holiday.

Here in his sea-girt realm, mid balmy gales,
Teased by no wire and only monthly mails,
High in his tree-clad seat above the wave
He holds such court as crowned kings might crave ;
While ladies fair, though few, with fitting grace
Share and refine the genius of the place.
Here Cadell's converse, Tuson's liquid song
Enhance the charm and speed the hours along ;
Where all were glad and making others glad——
Years will not dim the pleasant time we had.

Right well his Captains seconded their Chief ;
There at the ebb we visited the reef,
Plucked the fair coral blossoms where they grew
So pink, so white, so delicately blue.
We saw the little jail on Viper's shore
For those who, once admonished, erred once more ;
(It seemed to need the few who were not free
To emphasise the general liberty ;)
We saw some natives, half reclaimed and rude,
Adorned with shells, but desperately nude ;
There bought we bows and sea-shells one and all,
And sheaves of arrows, trophies for the hall ;
We saw the tea-house, drank the fragrant tea
From plants that were but seeds in '83 ;

While every reach and every headland passed
Revealed some vista lovelier than the last.

    Thence to Camorta, where I fished in vain ;
A monster broke me and was off again ;
Alas ! I have no details of the trip
For illness held me prisoner by the ship.
Yet did I shake a friendly hand with Man
Who anthropologizeth when he can,
And knows and almost loves the Andaman.
(He vowed by all the Andaman religions
He'd send me up a pair of bronze-winged pigeons.)*
I have his book, and contemplate the pleasure
Of mastering the language—at my leisure.

    Back to Port Blair, and onward to Rangoon
Athirst for war news ; and we heard full soon
The loud salute resounding through the bay
For Theebaw caught and taken Mandalay.

    Ashore I found my friend of early years
Now judging in Rangoon, my trusty Meres ;
While kind MacEwen opened his abode
And held high hospital in Halpin Road.

---

* And he kept his vow, but they died on the voyage.

There Griffiths, master of the healing art,
Most patient man of ear, and kind of heart,
Did something like a miracle display—
He all but cured me in a single day.
Long may he flourish in his chosen line!
The thanks be his; the benefit is mine.

So to Port Blair once more. Nay, do not pout!
My Muse, like you, fair reader, is tired out;
I will but note the kindness and good-will
That all untiring lighted on us still
And urge on all who need a change of air
The round,—Rangoon, Camorta, and Port Blair;
And to that end as swiftly as I can
Shall take this copy to the "Englishman."

SONG.

THE breath of morn came soft,
    The sunlight kissed the lea ;
The skylark soared aloft
    And carolled wild and free ;
As sunlight to the skylark
    So I would be to thee !

Noon hushed the ring-doves' cooing ;
    I was not there to see,
But I heard about their wooing
    From the honey-laden bee ;
As shadow to the ring-doves
    So I would be to thee !

'T was night ; the moonbeams glistened
    On nightingale and tree ;
The rose awoke and listened
    And loved the melody ;
As nightingales to roses
    So I would be to thee !

PRESENCE OF MIND.

JACK was smart and witty ;
    Fanny was a flirt,
Perilously pretty,
    Petulantly pert.

Jack alone one day
    With this merry Miss
(Who would not, you'll say)
    Stole a kiss.

Fan was nothing loth ;
    But the mischief in her
Made her peach, when both
    Sat at dinner,

Thinking Jack would blush ;
    Jack was not so weak ;
First he broke the hush—
    " Well, I like your cheek !"

WEDDING-DAY VERSES.
To S. M. B. (with a clock).

SWEET lady, twenty years have sped
    Mid twenty shifting scenes
Since erst I to the altar led
    The maiden in her teens.

And day by day some newer trait
    And nobler than before,
Has knit the tie that you and I
    Made fast in days of yore.

Nor least, though last, the nerve that passed
    Unshrinking o'er the wave
That life and joy might bless the boy
    Whose joyous life you gave!

Then, dearest Lady, in the name
    Of all our merry seven——
Aye, and of those who early rose
    To purer joys in heaven,——

This simple lay shall greet the day
    Beyond all others dear
Whose dawning light with pebble white
    Will mark the circling year.

God grant the gift to which you lift
    Your waking eyes to-morrow
May chime a thousand hours of joy
    To half an hour of sorrow.

YE STOUT MOUNTAINEER.
Darjiling, November 1884.

THOU who endeavourest
To see Mount Everest
Since thou wilt never rest
   Until thou see it——
Thee six stout men shall
Waft up to Senchal ;
If six can't, ten shall !
   Amen ! So be it !

Lest mists arising
Thy path surprising
Unsympathizing
   Obscure thy sight,
O thou who climbest
To peaks sublimest
See that thou timest
   Thy raid aright !

Then feast thine eyes on
The point that lies on
The far horizon
   Undisconcerted,
Nor miss the token
By sages spoken——
A sky-line broken
   By bowl inverted.

OLD CHITTAGONG.

Air.—We'll all go a-hunting to-day.

1.

AS you ask me to sing some original thing
   I suppose I can hardly be wrong
If I try to rehearse in appropriate verse
   The glories of Old Chittagong.
      Then, gentlemen, join in the song
      With a chorus to help it along ;
   'Tis the right of the host to lead off with a toast
      And I give you—our Old Chittagong.

2.

We have hills, we have plains, and such sweet winding
   lanes
   As to Devon and Dorset belong,
But the fern and the palm lend a tropical charm
   To the landscape of Old Chittagong.
      Then, gentlemen, join in the song, &c.

3.

The boats come and go in the river below
   And hither rich argosies throng,
For fortunes are made by the merchants who trade
   In our paddy and jute and souchong.
      Then, gentlemen, join in the song, &c.

4.

Each year of our lives more shipping arrives
    In our harbour at Old Chittagong,
And right gladly we meet, and right gaily we greet
    Our Nelson, Macpherson and Spong.
        Then, gentlemen, join in the song, &c.

5.

If by fever distressed or in need of a rest
    The Chaffinch will bear us along,
And J—o and C—x have a snug little box
    At the Simla of Old Chittagong.
        Then, gentlemen, join in the song, &c.

6.

Our society here is true and sincere
    And the bond of good fellowship strong;
Of a pique or a clique no one ventures to speak
    In our circle at Old Chittagong.
        Then, gentlemen, join in the song, &c.

7.

When we're due at our club for our set or our rub
    We need neither signal nor gong,
Nor regret if it's wet but just over the net
    Send the shuttlecock flashing along.
        Then, gentlemen, join in the song, &c.

8.

The ladies attend, and their countenance lend
  To our pastime at Old Chittagong ;
And there's one who presides and arranges our sides ;
  To them let me offer my song.
      Then, gentlemen, join in the song,
        With a chorus to help it along ;
      By the right of the host I will vary the toast
        To " The Ladies of Old Chittagong ! "

SWIMMING.

A GENTLEMAN said to his children two,
  He said to his son and his daughter,
You wouldn't know what upon earth to do
  If you tumbled into the water :
Now, the rains are here and the water is clear,
  Pleasant and fresh and brimming,
And that little green path leads down to the bath ;
  So who's for a lesson in swimming ?

You may float like a log, you may move like a dog,
  But if we can only find her,
The model for us is a slender frog
  With her legs thrown out behind her.

Swimming.

There! what a spring, like a thing on the wing;
    Merrily in she plunges;
If only one swims, one may lave one's limbs
    And a fig for soaps and sponges!

Please understand that a child on land
    Walks by alternate motion;
But you mustn't do so, you know, to go
    Through river or lake or ocean;
For the supple limbs of a person who swims
    Upper alike and nether
Must be closely pressed to the body and chest
    And struck out all together.

You will find it, I think, pretty easy to sink
    Without any previous notice;
So it won't be in vain if I deign to explain
    What the secret of keeping afloat is;
It turns upon this, young master and miss,
    That the body of son and daughter,
All but the face, must be made to displace
    An equal body of water.

If you yield to alarm and throw up each arm
    You'll just go bubbling under,

And then when you rise you'll goggle your eyes
    In a terrified stare of wonder.
Let none be a fool in the pool, but cool ;
    And this is the plan to go on ;
A breath and a stroke, like sensible folk,
    Float till the next, and so on.

Please look alive when you strive to dive ;
    For the rule according to Cocker
Is to cleverly point your hands and head
    Towards Davy Jones's locker ;
Butt with your head, pray with your hands,
    Open your eyes as you travel,
For fear of a shock from a block of rock
    Or a nose well grazed on the gravel.

Pray have a care if a hand you bear
    To save a friend from sinking ;
Some practice first ere it comes to the worst
    Is worth a deal of thinking ;
'Tis a dangerous task ; though I would not ask
    To have my children shirk it ;
If he clasps you round you'll both be drowned
    So I'll tell you how to work it.

I'd see him well spent before I went,
  Just paddling at some distance,
Or punch his head till he lay like dead
  And open to assistance;
Then tow him with care by his clothes or hair;
  Or his ear, by way of variety;
So hauling him in the medal you'll win
  Of the Royal Humane Society!

WITH MY GUN.

FAREWELL to the crowded city,
  Farewell to the Bench and Bar;
O bear with my doggrel ditty
  As I sally forth afar!

I feel a fine compassion
  For the jaded form and mien
Of the finikin sons of fashion,
  And the daughters of routine.

I hold the ball of the cartridge
  Assembly balls above;
And the call of the early partridge
  Is the morning call I love.

A SHIPWRECK ON SHORE.*

"Dare Carbasa Vento."

1.

A GENTLEMAN lived on Fairy Hill,
   He and his family too ;
But his landlord treated them all so ill
   They didn't know what to do :
Fair wear and tear he wouldn't repair,
   This unbelieving Jew,
Not even a patch for the hole in the thatch
   Where the rain came trickling through :
And yet he was bent on raising the rent
   To double the sum he drew !
So the gentleman went to live in a tent
   He and his family too.

2.

Father and Mother and Harry and Vi
   And a baby plump to see
With as pink a face and as sweet a grace
   As a baby's well could be ;
Chickens and cow, rabbits and geese,
   Ponies and dogs galore,
Which Topsy, the beast, at length increased
   By ten little puppy-dogs more ;
So the rabbits played and the ponies neighed
   And the cow made answer " Moo-ooh ! "
Content he spent his Lent in a tent
   He and his family too.

---

* The point of this rhyme rather lies in its genesis. On the morning after the storm, some kind friends came down to the ruins to offer their help. They found the writer under a tree, and the rhyme completed. *Après le deluge—Moi !*

তাম্বুবাস।

১

জনেক সাহেব সপরিবার
ভাড়া লইলেন প'র পাহাড়;
ট্যাশ ফিরিঙ্গীর মাটী ছিল,
যার পর নাই সে কষ্ট দিল;
দিন দিন করিল ছল,
রাত রাত পড়িল জল;
মাস মাস কসে লয় ভাড়া,
দিতেও নারিল একটী নাড়া;
তবে টাকা লোভের বলে
চাহিল দুই শত একের স্থলে;
দিতে না পারিয়া, ধর্ম্মাবতার
তাম্বুতে যাইলেন সপরিবার।

২

কর্ত্তা গৃহিণীর দুই জন ছেলা
অতি সুশীলা করিত খেলা;
কোলের খুকী, কমলমুখ,
দেখিতে সুন্দর, নয়নের সুখ;
গোরু ঘোড়া খাইত ঘাস;
চাল জল পাইত হাঁস;
দুই গুণ হইল কুকুরের ফল,
দশটা বাচ্ছা, কেমন দল;
খরগোস খেলে ঘোড়া ঘোড়া;
গো করে হাম্বা, চিঁহিঁ করে ঘোড়া;
তুষ্ট হইলেন ধর্ম্মাবতার
ফাল্গুন মাসে সপরিবার।

3.

His eldest daughter had lately wed,
    She and her husband too ;
Happy indeed was the life they led
    With the honeymoon hardly through ;
But she cried, as she pined for the baby plump
    And the chicks and the parent pair,
" Let us visit a spell where the old folk dwell,
    If they have any pied-à-terre !"
And the old man cried, " Make way for the bride
    And her Guernsey lad !" cried he ;
So he readily lent the dining tent
    And they dined out under a tree.

4.

He wrote for a right to the building site
    But the time flew quickly past ;
Really it seemed that the family dreamed
    These halcyon days would last :
The nights as a rule were clear and cool,
    The noondays rather warm ;
But didn't the gentleman look like a fool
    When the whole came down in a storm
Totter and crash ! shiver and smash !
    O what a piteous view !
Ruin around and he half-drowned,
    He and his family too.

৩

সাহেবের কন্যা, নবনারী,
গিয়াছিলেন স্বামীর বাড়ী ;
নূতন বাড়ী স্থাপন করিল,
সুখেও কাল যাপন করিল ;
তবে মনে উঠিল দুখ ;
" ছোট বোন দেখিব নয়নের সুখ ;
বাপের বাড়ী যাইব, নাথ !
এক্ষণে চল তাম্বুর নাঠ।"
পিতা শুনিয়া তুষ্ট হন ;
স্থান অভাবে উভয় জন
রাখে তাম্বুর আহারঘরে ;
গাছের তলে আহার করে।

৪

সাহেব কুঠী দিতে চায় ;
ক্রমে ক্রমে সময় যায় ;
এইটী কি সিদ্ধান্ত হবে,
বারনাস বসন্ত রবে ?
রাতে শীত নরম নরম,
দিনে রৌদ্র গরম গরম ;
শেষে সন্ধ্যায় উঠিল ঝড়,
ভাঙ্গিয়া পড়িল কাপড়ের ঘর !
লজ্জিত হইল সাহেবের মন,
ছিন্ন ভিন্ন সাহেবের ধন,
মগ্ন হইল জিনিষ তাঁর,
তিনিও মগ্ন, সপরিবার।

5.

Dozens of beer, so dear out here,
  Shattered and spilt and spent;
And the crystal lamp, the pride of the camp,
  Down with the rest it went:
And worse, alas! the glittering glass
  That a steed might well reflect
Is lying in fragments sharp and small
  Totally, utterly wrecked;
Then, alas! for the glass so tall and brave
  With its fondly flattering view!
Where the gentleman always stood to shave——
  He and his family too.

6.

Many a chair in crushed despair
  The carpenter's aid must beg:
Many a table hitherto stable
  Limps on a broken leg:
Never a clock but felt the shock
  And down it came with a thud;
Never a dress unless in a mess,
  Muddle and puddle and mud;
His bedding is wet and his plans upset;
  He must furnish his house anew;
And now he repents of living in tents,
  He and his family too.

৫

বিয়ার শ্যাম্‌কিন্‌ অতি দুর্ম্মূল্য
মাঠে বহিল জলের তুল্য ;
চূর হইল, দেখে ধনী,
কাচের ফানস, তাম্বুর মণি ;
চূর হইল, কেমন কষ্ট,
* " অশ্ব দর্পণ " সুন্দর, মস্ত ;
ভাল দেখিতে যেমন সুখ,
ভগ্ন দেখিতে তেমনি দুখ ;
কেন না, ইহাতে ধর্ম্মাবতার
দাড়ি কামাইতেন সপরিবার।

৬

কেদেরা যেরূপ ভাঙ্গিল, তা
বিনা সুতারে উঠিবে না ;
বিপদে পড়িয়া মেজ্‌ চারপায়
কেবল খঞ্জের ন্যায় খোঁড়ায় ;
হঠাৎ যখন উঠিল ঝড়ি,
ধপ্‌ করে পড়িল তিনটী ঘড়ী ;
চারি দিকে কাদা কিচা,
কাপড় বিছানা তাবৎ ভিজা ;
নূতন জিনিষ নিতে হবে,
অনেক টাকা দিতে হবে ;
তাম্বুবাসে ধর্ম্মাবতার
ক্লান্ত হইলেন, সপরিবার।

---

* অর্থাৎ দাড়া আশি।

ADIEU.

O GENTLE astronomer Strahan!*
    Your Steamer is off with the dawn;
  The melody lingers
  That flowed from your fingers
But ah! the performer is gone.

For Strahan, as our suffrages show,
Is the right sort of fellow to know;
  His skill with the racquet
  Invites one to back it,
And think how he handles the bow!

When Pinafore wouldn't go right
Rehearsed on the critical night
  The brave became grave
  At so narrow a shave
But he was all hopeful and bright.

True heart—and a love for Mozart
Of his merits are only a part;
  For merry and fair
  Are they who declare
He likes to give lessons in art.

---

* Major G. Strahan, R.E., of the Great Trigonometrical Survey, paid us a visit. It was a transitory one.

Alas! you are off with the dawn;
We shall miss you at four on the lawn:
　But you'll think now and then
　Of this oddest of men
And his rhyme on astronomer Strahan?

THE BAGGED JACKAL.

HURRAH for the horn and the hound!
　Hurrah for the burst and the bound!
Hurrah for the hunt and the quarry in front,
The quarry our Halliday found.

For fear the unfortunate scamp
Should nibble a hole and decamp,
To baffle his hopes they bound him with ropes
And may be he suffered from cramp.

All booted and bridled and spurred,
The upshot was worse than absurd;
The bobbery pack had eaten the jack
Before he could utter a word.

TWENTY O'CLOCK!

I CANNOT exactly say how it arises—
I'm always the victim of startling surprises;
And now I've just suffered a terrible shock!
I'm asked out to dinner at twenty o'clock!

I'm an elderly man, of conservative turn,
Content to remember, not eager to learn;
I like institutions as firm as a rock;
What ails her to talk about twenty o'clock?

We prate about progress; it flatters our pride;
Yet we are but the playthings of cycle and tide;
We only return, if the truth be admitted,
To walk in the ways that our grandfathers quitted.

When clocks were invented, they made them to chime
From one up to twenty-four hours at a time;
And cuckoos, who cuckoo two dozen at a go
Still linger, I hear, in the Canton of Vaud.

A truce to lamenting! It's vain to repine;
The world will not alter its notions for mine;
So listen a little, and let me take stock
Of things atavistic like twenty o'clock.

I hear Sarah Battle inviting the throng
Short whist to abandon in favour of long ;
While Handel in smiles from a corner in heaven
Sees Sullivan's score on a stave of eleven.

Ere long shall the glory of Oscar be past
With pseudo-æsthetics too sickly to last ;
And artists like those of a healthier age
Paint lilies and roses for sun-flower and sage.

Nor less will our sportsmen, if worthy the name,
Vote battues and beaters unmanly and tame ;
And a flask and slow matches for cartridge and cock
Will find us a pheasant for twenty o'clock.

The dinner I'm asked to, I'm able to state,
Will be plainer and better than dinners of late ;
And ale and metheglin, not Chablis or Hock,
Will wash down our sirloin at twenty o'clock.

It's striking nineteen! I must send for my man,
And hasten my dressing, and hail a sedan ;
I'm off! at the door of my hostess to knock
At exactly five minutes to twenty o'clock.

ACROSTIC TO A LADY.

LADY, awake! for thy star-browed steed
   I wis had never as fair a freight;
Zephyr is playing o'er mountain and mead;
   Zephyr still toys with his early mate;*
Into the saddle while day is new,
Ere sunshine kisses away the dew.

Lady, arise! for thy star-browed steed
   Eagerly champs on his idle bit;
Vault o'er the brook with a falcon's speed,
   Image of grace, with thine Arab knit;
Enter these lines in thine album, pray,
Nor blame the bold poet who penned the lay.

ANSWER TO JEANNIE.

(I wish I could give my readers the charming song to which the following is an answer. But it is not mine, but the work, I believe, of a Scotch lady, and has not,

---

   * "Zephyr with Aurora playing,
      As he met her once a-maying."

as far as I know, been published. The lassie asks her mither what she must say when ' Jamie comes to woo.')

    JEANNIE, has he loved ye long?
        Dare ye trust his vow?
    Has he wooed and lightly left
        Or never loved till now?
    Lassie! is he brave and kind,
        Strong and leal and true?
    Gin he be, ye need na frown
        When Jamie comes to woo.

    Is he wise and thoughtful aye,
        Full of quiet power?
    Will he shield from every blast
        My little Higieland flower?
    Lassie! is he brave and kind,
        Strong and leal and true?
    Gin he be, ye munna frown
        When Jamie comes to woo.

    Lassie! nestle nearer yet!
        Has he won your heart?
    Is it sunlight when ye meet
        And shadow when ye part?

Then, gin he be brave and kind,
  Strong and leal and true,
Jeannie smile! and Heaven shall smile
  On Jamie and on you.

TO M. Ff-M., BANYAN LODGE.

FOR apt intonation and musical trill
  No minas are equal to those of the hill;
I know of a hill by a banyan protected
Which a Mina in building her nest has selected;
Her mate may well listen with pleasure and pride
As she sings to her sweet little nestling inside,
For there is not a hill throughout India or China
With a cosier nest or a cleverer mina.

A FANFARONADE

On a clever sketch of a young lady, whose fancy dress and suite of ornaments were entirely designed after a Fan pattern.

O MAID of most enchanting fancy!
  Deny me if you can
The right with strictest relevancy
  To call you simply——Fan.

A Fanfaronade.

The lands of mangosteen and mango
    With China and Japan
Have vied to grace your gay fandango,
    Fair phantom, with a fan.

Your dress, too—though of ladies' dresses,
    Your lover, as a man,
Frankly his ignorance confesses—
    Dear Fan, is *diaphane*.

New-fangled though your glories, Fanny,
    And Vanity of Vanity,
To hint at such a thought uncanny,
    My Fanny, were profanity.

Then fairest Fan, and fanniest fair,
    By Zephyr and by Venus
Make oath and swear you will take care
    No coolness rise between us.

Mine are your every air and motion,
    An heirloom too ecstatic;
And I lie prostrate in devotion,
    For I am your fanatic.

A BURST OF SONG.

THE lady was a pianiste
    Of credit and renown;
And gaily ran she up the keys
    And gaily ran she down;

Nor only in her instrument
    The lady did rejoice;
For wedded with the harpsichord
    Rang out her tuneful voice.

A gallant youth behind her stood
    Whose cornet pure and clear
Did tootle too entirely too
    Entrancing to the ear;

A *preux chevalier*, in whose veins
    Blent by a happy chance
There ran the mingled gallantry
    Of England and of France;

A knight whose knightly courtesy
    Would mark him in a crowd;
For if a lady passed, he rose;
    And if she smiled, he bowed.

Anon she singeth ; and anon
    The knight he tootleth ;
But since, you see, a full deep note
    Requires a full, deep breath,

The lady rising to the note
    A full deep breath she drew ;
When lo ! from off her bodice trim
    Seven hapless buttons flew !

Three lay upon the ivory keys,
    Three rolled among their toes ;
And one rebounding reached the knight
    And struck him on the nose.

Now knights of England and of France
    So blamelessly behave,
No comic *contretemps* can make
    Their courtesy less grave.

And yet I wis that gallant gay
    With conflict dire was torn ;
What lips that lengthen to a smile
    Can tootle on a horn ?

He did not laugh, he did not smile,
    He resolutely played ;

But ah! the curious quavering note
    His merriment betrayed!

The lady laughed both loud and long;
    Then laughed the knight outright;
Yet did he speedily regain
    His manner most polite.

" O gracious lady! For that laugh
    "'A thousand thanks,' he cried;
" For hadst thou kept thy countenance
    " I had not laughed, but died!"

Now be our song " The Queen live long!
    " The lady long live she;
" And when her bodice next doth burst
    " May we be there to see!"

———

"OFF VENICE."

1.

SILENT the city slumbers afar,
　Lightly thy fingers wake the guitar;
Softly the moonbeams melt in the sea,
Fondly thy dark eyes linger on me.

2.

Thou art my moon, love, I am thy deep,
Sink on my bosom calmly to sleep;
Slowly our Gondola drifts with the tide,
Dreamily, endlessly, thus would I glide.

Original Epigrams.

IN CAROLUM DUBIUM TICHBORNUM.

MOLLITOS olim Phryne nudata dicastas
    Eximiâ formâ vicit, et erubuit.
Hic, duplicem duplici nudans cum corpore mentem,
    Nec causam obtinuit, crede, nec erubuit.
Mox lictor, rursus nudato in verbera tergo,
    Dixerit " Hic lorum sensit, et erubuit!"

FRAUS PIA.

DICITUR abscissis nullâ non fraude capillis
    Dallila præfortem despoliâsse virum;
Me meliore dolo cepit dulcissima conjux
    Scilicet abscissis crinibus ipsa suis.

SIMILIA SIMILIBUS.

PULVERE tu gaudes; fumi mihi gratior umbra;
    Quid rides? ipsi pulvis et umbra sumus.

Translations thereof.

THE UNFORTUNATE NOBLEMAN.

WHEN lovely Phryne stood revealed,
    The jurors could but gaze and yield ;
The accusing counsel's voice was hushed ;
Thus Phryne won her cause, and blushed.

His double bulk till Tichborne peeled,
His double dealing lay concealed ;
Soon as he stripped, his hopes were crushed,
He lost his cause, but never blushed.

Yet, if he pass the prison-door,
The law may bid him strip once more ;
The lash provoke a genuine flush,
And teach the claimant how to blush.

TO A LADY WITH SHORT HAIR.

THEY tell us that Dalilah, faithless and fair,
    Made conquest of Samson by cutting his hair ;
If Dalilah only the secret had known
She'd have conquered him sooner by cutting her own.

LIKE TO LIKE.

OURSELVES we are but dust
    And ashes, it's allowed ;
Take snuff, Sir, if you must,
    And I will blow my cloud

ACTUS CURIÆ.

A LEARNED brother, now alas! no more
    Loved quips and cranks, and kept a goodly store;
Nor thought it scorn, as meaner men have done,
To point his weighty wisdom with a pun.
This puisne judge a puny dog had bred,
Which followed faithful where its master led,
And when my comrade sought the judgment seat,
Crept into court, and nestled at his feet.
A junior counsel whispered " With our Daniel
A spaniel comes to judgment! yea, a spaniel!"
Poor Smith! his habit was to tilt his chair,
Its forelegs nicely balanced in the air,
Emblem of all a judge's mind should be
When poised between dismissal and decree.
Once counsel, canvassing with serious face
The precedents that ruled his client's case,
Broke off in citing Blaggins *v.* Blogg—
" Your Lordship's chair will crush your Lordship's dog!"
" ' Nay, fear not, brother,' quoth poor Smith, "for see——
" ' Nullum gravabit actus curiæ.'"

UNIVERSITY SCHOLARSHIPS, 1855.

WHEN Holmes made good the double fight,
　　This paradox befel:
A Craven scholar proved his right
　　To bear away the Bell.

FANCY DRESS.

OUR Mephistopheles arose
　　Clad from the knees in silken hose.
The man was long and lean of figure,
The hose were made for some one bigger.
Quoth Faust, " Your stockings seem to stand
" Like Israel on the desert sand;
" Miss the fat calves, nor rest within
" The weary wilderness of Shin!"

TO MY DAUGHTER.

SWEET birdie, when our hearts are gay
　　And all is joy and peace,
You pipe and trill the livelong day
　　A Nightingale of Nice.
But when the couch of pain is spread
　　And cheeks you love grow pale,
You hover round the sufferer's bed
　　A Florence Nightingale!

WRITTEN ON THE BACK OF A MENU CARD AT TABLE D'HÔTE.

[A beautiful lady, evidently a bride, had sat near us for some days. One evening she appeared with a guest as fair as herself.]

C'EST pour le voyageur une belle fortune
S'il trouve en se tournant vers le ciel une lune ;
Et ce soir notre sort est encore plus heureux
En voyant cet azur illuminé de deux !

ON AN ENGRAVING OF THE REVEREND WILLIAM KNIBB, AN ANTI-SLAVERY REFORMER, WRITING.

A PEN without a nib is idle,
And like a horse without a bridle :
A nib without a pen is worse,
And like a bridle with no horse :
Therefore, to make the perfect feather,
Knibb and his pen are drawn together.

ON A STATION IN LOWER BENGAL.

OUR Church as at present it stands
    Has no congregation, nor steeple ;
The lands are all low-lying lands
    And the people are low lying people.

THE KILT.

OUR Hielander Fergus Macleod
    Appeared of his petticoats proud ;
For these and his sporran
Looked stylish and foreign,
And this Mrs. Muggins allowed.

AT THE EDEN GARDENS.

OUR gardeners through the changing day
    In varying tools delight ;
We see the hose each morning play ;
    The rakes come out at night.

LOCAL SELF-GOVERNMENT.

WHEN Chantrey's woodcocks graced the double toast
    He carved the pair and sent them to his host.
We miss the art our fathers used to teach,
They formed their bodies with a Beak to each ;
But Colman's game would baffle Chantrey's skill,
A hundred headless bodies and one Bill.
Fat were the feast, and rich the groaning salver
Could all be trophies of some modern Carver !

STEADY UNDER FIRE.

[The Bankura Fire-Brigade, a beneficent hobby of the District Officer, had a complete military organization. It was burning to see active service, but in vain ; till a fire, with true native tact, broke out in the house of the *Sarishtadar*, and was promptly extinguished.]

CALEDONIA had never a grander son
    Than our doughty Collector Jock Anderson ;
      See where he comes
      With his banners and drums
Leading his bold Salamanders on !

PROMOTION BY MERIT.

WHERE kin or friendship gives a lien
    Surpassing merit is detected;
Which, teste Darwin, comes to mean
    Extinction of the unselected.

A MATRIMONIAL NOTICE, "SMITH—ARMOUR."
EPIGRAM THEREON.

"Arma virumque cano."

THEY tell us since Vulcan's original myth
    That all coats of armour are made by a Smith;
But now that the chaplain has married his charmer
We meet with a Smith newly made of an Armour.

ON A SIMLA SCANDAL.

WHEN David fell victim to Bathsheba's charms
    Uriah the Hittite was ordered to arms;
But now the offender bears justly the brunt
And only the villain is sent to the front.

ON A MEMBER OF OUR MAGAZINE CLUB.

"He kept the numbers as the numbers came."

TRIFLES.

A CRITIC cried, "Mid peaceful scenes
  "What martial arts I use!
"In charge of several magazines
  "And always at reviews!"

I've heard an old humourist tell
That a cause is akin to a bell;
The truth of which saying you feel
When it comes to be heard in appeal.

"A judge unrobe in public?" "Yes, my brother,
"You put a rent suit off and try another."

LEARNED COUNSEL.
(*Chittagong*, 1883.)

LET the public support
  The Bar in this Court;
Our T. A. P. is uncommonly good.
But if you don't find
The said Tap to your mind
You may take a long pull from the Wood.

LONG DISCOURSES.

A BURMAN devout buys a manuscript prayer
And prays it by slinging it high in the air.
Our Rector might borrow a hint from the Burmans
And nail to the pulpit his prosier sermons.

ON A METRONOME.

THIS little click-devil
Requires to be level.

TAKING THE CUE.

BROWN played a cannon, but instead
Just missed the white and fluked the red;
"'How fine a cut!' cried Brown in clover,
"You saw how neatly it heeled over?"
"'It heeled,' said Spriggins, as you mention,
"But hardly by the first intention."

A FACT.

I CAUGHT three tiny fish
  And told my tiny son
That two would meet my wish
  And he should feast on one.
" Now this is most unfair,"
  Replied the little prig ;
" You take the larger share
  " And how can I grow big ?"

DEDICATED TO THE TENT CLUB.

HE whose 12-bore o'er-bore the boar
  Which he forbore to ride,
Himself a bore, destroyed a boar,
  Committing ——— suicide.

VIRO DOCTISSIMO J. P. GRANT.

QUI Sitagoniacis donabas nuper in oris
  Tanta viatori munera, Munus eris.

POOL.

IN frequently playing at pool
    With a pseudo-homonymous friend,
I ran the man close, as a rule,
    But always got slain in the end.
One player was destined to sell,
    The other was doomed to be sold;
The name of the one was Bignell
    And the name of the other—Bignold.

TO R. H. GREAVES, ESQ., B.C.S.

HIM will I right, if writing can,
    Of whom an erring world believes
He is a melancholy man
And always grieves, and only grieves!
For well doth childish praise appraise
His kindly ways and playful wiles;
And, cast among congenial traits,
He cannot help himself, but smiles.

THE AMATEUR PRINTER.

> 'So careful of the type!'
> *Tennyson.*

THESE lines a Printer-poet chose
    From either fount to pick;
These the composer did compose
    And printed off his stick.

A BOAST.

WE printers are a sporting race;
    This line I'll justify;
We're given to shooting and the chase
    And find ourselves in pie.

DECLARATION UNDER ACT XXV OF 1867.

THE tiny press whose arbiter I am
    Will charm a child, or fix an epigram:
If maxims hold, and minims claim no heed,
The courts will reck but little of my deed;
Yet—for I would not that the law were broken—
I do declare the fact. Be this my token.

PROLOGUE

To be spoken by BETSY BAKER.

" BETSY BAKER! (*curtsey*) at your service!" (*curtsey*).

WHEN the Honeymoon's ended and over,
    Too smooth a devotion may cloy,
Inducing a surfeit of clover,
    A quite too unbearable joy.

You shall see our young Benedict Mouser
    Preserve such a Darby-like tone
That at last Mrs. Mouser avows her
    Reluctance to posing as Joan.

Till Crummy, a kindly relation,
    Not wishing the potion to pall,
Devises a small complication
    For mixing a relish of gall.

So I'm to make love to young Mouser
    And deftly her Darby ensnare,
By which we expect to arouse her
    To jealousy, wrath and despair.

And Crummy, if nothing miscarries,
    Declares ere the curtain shall drop
He'll marry me off to young Harris
    And buy us a Greengrocer's shop!

EPILOGUE TO

"DEAREST MAMMA."

December 28th, 1880.

DEAR Friends, the trifle we present
   Is all we have to offer :
A dish of modest merriment,
   No challenge to the scoffer.

We know, kind audience, you've a heart
   So chivalrous in tone
It needs must take that actor's part
   Who cannot take his own.

No garb laborious we prepare,
   But put a casual stitch in,
At moments which we ill can spare
   From cradles, courts, and kitchen.

Our craft has made no easy trip,
   The waves had nearly swamped her ;
And if we've saved the little ship
   We owe it to—
     (*Jones from R. Wing*)......" The Prompter ! "

We see our newly married pair
   Their happy tents out-spreading ;
Around them hangs, a halo fair,
   The glamour of the wedding.

Old uncle finds a cosy shelf;—
    A man inured to suffer
His late lamented dearer self—
    A better half, but rougher.
        (*Croker*)............"*Poor* buffer!!"

But now that troublous tongue is dumb,
    He counts his trials over;
Preserves his equilibrium
    And ruminates in clover;

Till all must yield in evil hour
    Beatitude for bustle,
And trembling own the awful power
    Of—(*Mrs. B. F.*)...... " Mrs. Breezely Fussel!"

While honest Jones in injured tones
    Denounces her vagaries,
And Mary Jane is half insane
    Chaffed by the neighbouring areys.

The cynic finds his subtlest joys
    In plotting to provoke her;
And she her talons well employs
    In nettling Nettle Croker.

Meanwhile that widow fresh and fair
    Seems safely booked to pin him,
But finds on cracking him with care
    That he has nothing in him!
      (*Mrs. H.*)...... " I'll win him !! "

The moral then, dear matrons, is,
    When once your chits are wedded,
Don't let them think a mother's phiz
    A terror to be dreaded;

But come and pass a pleasant day;
    Don't worry or oppose 'em
Nor longer stay; but slip away
    To cousin Towzler's bosom.

And Harry! when her mother comes,
    Be careful not to rouse her;
But yield, and smile, and twirl your thumbs—
    And leave the rest to
      (*Uncle B.*)............... " Browser !!! "

EPILOGUE TO
"ICI ON PARLE FRANCAIS."

(Played in our Billiard Room.)

WE'VE moved the old table,
  But hope we've been able
    To show you our play all the same;
That no canon dramatic
Has found us erratic,
  Or wanting in strength or in aim.

We own that the ball
Must come off in the hall,
  To vary the act and the scene;
Content if we use
Our appropriate cues,
  Though our room, not our table, be green.

When Victor the lover,
Intent to discover
  The lady-love torn from his eyes,
Comes gallantly over
From Calais to Dover,
  What droll complications arise!

Epilogue to Ici on Parle Francais.

Our Julia trim,
Though wedded to him
   Who could hardly be sterner or stricter,
Having stolen a march
Is inclined to be arch
   And flirt rather freely with Victor.

But Victor! beware
Of your protegée fair
   As she munches dry buns in the train;
For Major Rattan
Is a murderous man
   And chief of the children of Cane.

Ze dodge of old Spreeggins
For letting his deegins
   Ye seemple may sérve to surpraise;
Ze old hombog's unable
To strife against Babel
   But is n't he fon ven he traise!

Poor Anna Maria
Has plenty to try her
   In serving so motley a troupe;
She's druv to despair
With Mossou's pongs-de-terre
   The coffee—the boots—and the soup.

Epilogue to Ici on Parle Francais.

Says Spriggins " I offer—
My service I proffer!"
   (The martyr not moving a muscle);
A smile it may raise
That Julia's stays
   Should move Mrs. Spriggins's bustle!

Ze fair Angélina——
But ah! you have seen herr!
   To paint herr vas labour in vain;
——When Victor once marries
He'll take her to Paris
   And sketch us, like Monsieur de Taine.

But what were our play
Though we conned it all day,
   Rehearsing it most of the night,
Unless we could find
An audience kind,
   Sympathetic, and smiling and bright?

Your partial applause
Has filled every pause,
   And cheered our small comedy through;
So, now we must part,
From ze depse of my heart
   I veesh you—von fine ' how d'you do!'

EPILOGUE TO
"BOOTS AT THE SWAN."

(Written after the event, for a Rival Company.)

DEAR Friends, we have strutted an hour on the stage
    (Or jumped it, or reeled it, or rolled it);
A convict all funk and a peeler all drunk,
    And you have been here to behold it!

And as for our play, it was lively and gay;
    And surely, kind public, thou knowest
'Twere folly to try any subject too high
    When our talents incline to the lowest.

For he may well shine in painting a sign
    Who would merit no tribute from Ruskin;
And folks may get on in "Boots at the Swan,"
    Who would cygnally fail in the Buskin.

Admit that Frank Friskly in gossiping briskly
    Much pickle and beef could demolish,
That Pipkin would dally with sweets and with Sally,
    Nor say that our Boots wanted polish.

Our Lesbian's rhyme will live for all time,
    The romance she is writing, for ever ;
Her tresses are new and her stockings are blue
    And her acting decidedly clever.

Our beau with the name was a trifle too tame,
    And Emily, theme of his passion,
Averred she preferred (a small bird overheard)
    To be wooed in a livelier fashion.

And the maid—! Ah the maid seemed born to her trade,
    So sprightly and handy and smiling ;
Her part was too slight for an actress so bright,
    And manners so gaily beguiling.

You were charmed with the scene in its border of green ;
    You were charmed with the heat, which was howling ;
Khits, bearers, and bobbies so crowded the lobbies
    And a man with a bouquet for D——ling.

Now fearing no scoff we move merrily off
    Who came with much nervousness on ;
And all that we ask as the meed of our task ;
    Is: Remember the "Boots at the Swan."

PROLOGUE TO
"THE AREA BELLE."

THIS room you perceive is a kitchen,
 A snug little kitchen in town;
And I am my mistress's servant——
 Your servant (*curtseys*), Penelope Brown.

My smiles are as bright as my covers;
 So don't be surprised when I state
That a merry succession of lovers
 Comes down by the area gate.

My Pitcher is true to his duty,
  444 B.,
A man who knows something of beauty,
 To judge by his fondness for me.

My gay grenadier's an Apollo
 In bearskin,—it makes my heart bleed
To think that so many should follow
 Where one, only one, can succeed.

Poor Chalks too, he finds me enthralling,
 But a milkman is barely genteel;
He may call——in the way of his calling—
 But never sit down to a meal.

I wonder he bears with my fancies
    And woos one so cold and so proud ;
But Chalks's are honest advances
    And milkmen not easily cowed.

Oh crikey ! if good Mrs. Croaker
    Should happen to catch us at play—
But for fear we should chance to provoke her
    We wait till the cat is away.

For if lovers are wanting to kiss us,
    And we are inclined to be kissed,
It can 't be no business of Missus
    Perwided no mutton is missed.

But a pepperpot stands on the dresser ;
    A favourite signal of mine ;
She ha'n't no idea on it, bless her !
    As that pepperpot stands for a sign.

But again, there's the imminent danger
    Of two looking in at a time,
And each falling foul of a stranger ;
    O wouldn't the crash be sublime !

So I guard against such a quandary
  When once an appointment is fixed,
By noting the fact in my diary;
  And now they can never get mixed.

But there—I have given you an inkling;
  I mustn't stop prating all day;
The Manager's bell is a-tinkling
  And I have to open the play.

EPILOGUE TO
"BOMBASTES FURIOSO."

Spoken by DISTAFFINA (*Mr.* PRITCHARD).

PATRONS, the farce that forms our closing show
Drew bumper houses seventy years ago;
And Rhodes, the play-wright of these playful pages,
True metal shows (like Sanders'* roads) for ages.

  Methinks, if tender love, pathetic woes,
If passion's promptings, all too deep for prose,
Have power to charm, an exquisite delight
Should be the guerdon of our toil to-night.

---

* Our Municipal Vice-Chairman.

Epilogue to Bombastes Furioso.

Nor blame our author's merriment, although it
Burlesques the pompous pride of many a poet;
The right is ours, as humble fellow-foolers,
To lash our writers' laches, and our Rulers'.

Oh would some scathing Satirist arise
To snipe-shoot modern folly as it flies!
And, following Ilbert to his Capuan hill
Slay—not his recreant body, but his Bill;
That Bill, endorsed by none, that bears his name,
Presented, not for honour, but for shame!
Nor spare that elder Bill, the Grand Old Bloke,
Whose Art, axe-ominous, with many a stroke,
Would hack and fell our stately British Oak.
Britannicus, or any other cuss,
Will find a nobler Premier among us,
A Boss who knows no meaner fault than fuss.

So to our plot; the stately Griskinissa
You never met, so you will never miss her;
Not so his would-be consort, Distaffina:
I only hope you like her now you've seen her (*posing*)
And truth to tell, believe it an you list,
Until to-night I never have been Miss-ed.
This skirt is awkward, so you won't be hurt
If I prefer—Ahem!—a divided skirt;

This wig is ricketty, these trappings vain;
Fain would I cry "Pritchard's himself again!"
—So one whose girth was great, and sword-belt shorter,
Regretted he was stout as well as Porter.

Which name recalls by mere association
An Operetta set in operation
That fairly earned, and won, our acclamation.
Wherefore we greet with sympathising hand
Our fellow-workers in a rival band;
To us the bays of eloquence belong;
To them the sweet pre-eminence in song;
Or rather, let the distribution be,
To us the solid earth, to them the sea!
(This is a most felicitous conception—
A gift from Terra to her brother Neptune!)

To them good speed. No quarter-deckorations
But sixteen-anna art—delineations—,
Drawn from a cooler clime 'neath milder orbs—
Bespeak our artist-guest, and name him—Forbes!
This mount I could—but won't—indite an ode on;
You know it's Swiss, or you would swear it was Snow(e)d on.
I sniff a joke, it shan't escape us, shall it?
We owe his brush encomiums and his palette.

Epilogue to Bombastes Furioso.

Yon audience-chamber, wainscoted in brown,
Is just an ordinary room in town;
But when we need a forest or a garden,
Hi presto! we're in Eden or in Arden.

Now shall my muse—for gratitude has sharpened her—
Sing our self-sacrificing friend, the carpenter;
And, long as scenes shall shift, and curtains rise,
Oh, rare Jack Johnson! laud thee to the———flies.

The moral then, young ladies, that we proffer;
Is this: be sure you don't refuse an offer;
Take warning from my fate, whose tactics sinister
Caught at a Monarch and so lost a minister.
Now go to bed; to rise from slumber sound
Refreshed as wounded heroes from the ground;
I only ask before you seek the balmy,
Three cheers for brave Bombastes——and the Army!

CHARADES.

1.

WHEN Prussia's sons her prowess proved,
    The bitter end o'erpast,
She spared the haunts the Muses loved,
    The treasures of my Last.
But when the Commune's brutal rage
    In reckless fury burst,
The heirlooms of a future age
    Were buried in my First.
Then, comrades, fill the sparkling bowl,
And pledge the Prussian in my Whole.

2.

Miss Kitty is pretty and pert;
    She looks on myself as her slave;
" Can you make a charade?" said the flirt;
    And this is the answer I gave :—
" My First is a beautiful bay;
    " My Last is a beautiful quay;
" My Second the ladies' delight,
    " And my Whole is—what you are to me."

3.

My First upon each cold grey stone
  That lines the lonely sea;
Or where the frolic strawberry roan
Frets at a bondage all unknown
  And struggles to be free;
My Second to the suppliant poor
Turned from the miser's closing door,
  Or meagre devotee;
My Whole with buttered toast galore,
  And Bessie making tea.

4.

A Charade without a First.

The hour of ten had come and passed
  Without her host the lady reckoned;
My Whole had failed to bring my Last,
  And left her in my Last and Second;
And thus it chanced that after all
My lady never graced the ball.

5.

Two syllables my First compose;
Two syllables my Second shows;
And yet it may be questioned whether
We number four when both together.
My First a Grecian athlete cast,
And psalms fell sweetly on my Last;
My Whole, whatever it may prove,
Begets more argument than love.

6.

And thus they passed the ancient mill
   And sat beneath the willow;
They gazed into the depths so still,
   And watched each petulant billow
Fringing the little stream that burst
Impatient of my First.
They sat beneath the willow's shade
   Till, as the youth grew bolder,
His heart's fond secret he betrayed,
   And this is what he told her:
"Long have I sighed yet feared to speak
   "By hope, by doubt perplexed;
"Dare I but ask the boon I seek?"—
   She softly said——my Next;
And o'er her cheek a flush then stole;
Its hue was lovely,——and my Whole.

7.

Selina Slow accused her beau
 Of flirting with her sister ;
Said she, "your face reveals the case,
 "I'm certain that you kissed her !
" Confession which conceals the worst
 " Is no confession reckoned ;
" So be my Whole if you my First,
 " And own that you my Second."
" 'Tis true," he cried, "your loving pride
 " I never more will injure ;
" Now tell me why this instant I
 " Resemble sugared ginger ? "

8.

Deep in my First are found
 My Second, a precious hoard ;
As a Whole we abound on the battle-ground
 And Staunton's mimic board.

DECAPITATIONS.

9.

COMPLETE, we entangle the prey we enclose;
Beheaded, we're Arctic and stand for your nose.
If you cut off our tip, we're a War God in Greek,
Who, beheaded, is wealth, (if a Roman should speak).
Two-thirds of which wealth, if the other depart,
Still part of its sum is the Latin for art.

10.

Born of a schoolboy's idle aim,
With waterfowl I kindred claim
In virtue only of a name.
Beheaded once, I'm much the same
But twice, the felon's soul I tame,
Or droop with an ingenuous shame;
And thrice, a sylvan monarch's name
I stand, the residue of flame.
Again—now silence cries the dame;
Once more—by general acclaim
I add a breath to Byron's fame.

II.

My whole is cunning to beguile
And mask its malice with a smile;
Or rides with easy bound and free
The trackless surges of the sea;
Or numbers in its guild the man
Who labours as an artisan;
Or guards in memory's secret page
The mysteries of a bygone age.
Behead me! floating as before
I choose, alas, my path no more;
But yield myself a helpless slave
To driving wind and dashing wave.
Behead again, I stand at worst
The better portion of my first;
And though I run before the wind
I cannot choose but lag behind.

ENIGMAS.

12.

A LEGAL indictment, an onset, a price,
A grave exhortation of holy advice,
And the powder and shot that exactly suffice.

13.

Dedicated to the Graces.

My first is a bee from your bonnet;
My second a neigh from your mare;
My third is the tea from your teapot;
And nightly I flit through the air.

My first is a bee from the comb;
My next in a feast will be found;
My last a bold lover will take
If you yield him two inches of ground;
But I and my brother are hardly a pair
For day is the time when I fly through the air.

14.

When hostile lances glint afar
I rouse the slumbering host to war;
And varying forms I wear;
A sword, I deal a fatal blow;
A staff, I lay the monarch low;
I shine a gem on maiden's brow;
I yield at lover's tender vow,
Or break in wild despair.

DOUBLE ACROSTICS.

15.

WE pride ourselves much on a beautiful trait;
We squander our lives as we wait, day by day,
On our wizened old mistress, the wealth of Cathay.

1. The kind of knowledge given to few
   Which guides the hand to bake or brew.
2. The lid beneath whose shelter small
   The fierce heat warms its watery wall.
3. The den wherein the iron lay
   Till blushing it was borne away.
4. The spoon which glitters bright and clear
   If solid silver be too dear.
5. The chamber where my lady's lips
   Close o'er the comfort that she sips.

16.

Ruck of unselected we—
Epithet of mystery.

1. Mark for many a rifle's aim,
2. Not so red till spring time came.
3. Pencilled we and deep blue-eyed.
4. Hungry, fat, unglorified.
5. Dwelling, or the host inside.

17.

Inscribed to the Members of our Station Club.

Yes, the play hour merrily passes;
Two for the lads, and one for the lasses.

1. I bore the warrior to the fray,
   Then rankling in his breast I lay!

2. Far fetched? Then haply worth a trial;
   No worse at least than bare denial.

3. I'm often blacker than my due
   But never gloomier than when blue.

4. A tip of many a tale am I,
   And misapplied to certainty.

5. In myth (and Smith) we move and prove
   But shady peers of those above.

6. The fountain seeks the mountain's aid
   To sing thy praise, relenting maid.

7. Hair or no hair, 'tis wrong to pull it;
   A gentle squeeze will plant the bullet.

8. 'Tis strange alone, as in the text;
   Not so, when coupled with my next.

9. Rhymes, magazines, a book, some figures,
   The co-efficients—or the niggers.

18.

What in the world is the meaning of this?

Querquedulæ Gangetis et laboribus
Ululant hilariter, nomen et mores agunt;
Similis reponit Yttrianos Kalliphon,
Et concinebat vacuitas zothecula;
Delia barbarica te Jovis-jurans amant,
Et xerolophi faciebat orandos iter.
Ad est, Palæstina.

AN ANGLER'S ALPHABET.

A WAS an Angler agog for the day ;
B was the Basket he bore for his prey ;
C was a Caddis that lived in a Case ;
D was a dear little delicate Dace ;
E was an Eel, and the Effort to skin it ;
F was his Float, bobbing twice in a minute ;
G was the grayling of Tennyson's lay,*
H was the Hackle that lured him astray ;
I was old Izaak, the Prince of our folly ;
J was his Jest, for our Angler was jolly ;
K was his Kettle, with plenty of bait ;
L was the Line he dropped early and late ;
M was the Minnow that played on his hook ;
N were the Notes that he made for his book ;
O were the Osiers he happened to know ;
P was a Pike that was lurking below ;
Q was the Quill, when it merrily played ;
R was the Roach that its motion betrayed ;
S was the Salmon, the Lord of the stream ;
T was the Trout, with its silvery gleam ;
U was an Unguent old Izaak invented ;
V was a Vale by our Angler frequented ;
W, his Wanderings by Exe and by Wye ;
Z was his Zeal ; he will fish till he die !

---

* " Here and there a trusty lout
And here and there a grayling."
— *Tennyson.*

AN ALPHABET OF BIRDS.

A WAS an Adjutant, bolting a frog ;
B was a Bittern that boomed in a bog ;
C was a coppled Canary in cage ;
D was a Duck with a stuffing of sage ;
E was an Eagle aloft in an eyrie ;
F was a Falcon as fast and as fiery ;
G was a Goose with a gander to marry it ;
H was a Hern with two Handsaws to harry it ;
I was an Ibis, impartial,* en prince ;
J was the poor little Jackdaw of Rheims ;
K was a Kingfisher, couldn't he dive !
L was a Linnet ; they limed it alive ;
M was a Magpie that chattered and stole ;
N was a Nightingale pouring its soul ;
O was the Owl that Minerva assumes ;
P was a Peacock parading its plumes ;
Q was a Quail as it cowered in the stubble ;
R was a Rail with a habitat double ;
S was a Snipe as it darted askew ;
T was a Teal with a winglet of blue ;
U a Upupa or Emu or Seamew ;
V was a Vulture ; what screams he could scream
W a Wren, with a dome and no spire ;   [you ;
X was a Xantholæm † (kindly enquire);
Y was a Yuhina (ask as before) ;
Z, a Zostera ; there ar'n't any more.

* "In medio tutissimus ibis."
† Major Marshall is responsible for the last three birds.

AN ALPHABET OF BEASTS.

A WAS an Ass that ate artichokes raw;
B was a Bull for a Bonheur to draw;
C was a Cat and her kittens a-bed with her;
D was the Dog, and the life that he led with her;
E was the Elephant Barnum would buy;
F was a Fox with the hounds in full cry;
G a Gazelle with her soft dark eye;
H was a Horse that went cantering by;
I was an Ibex aloft in the snows;
J was a Jackal that sang through his nose;
K was a Kangaroo over the seas;
L was a Leopard, with links, if you please;
M was a Mouse, with a weakness for cheese;
N was a Nilgao, or buffalo buck;
O an Opossum all down on its luck;
P was a Pig that could point to a figure;
Q was a Quagga, a donkey grown bigger;
R was a Rat, or a Rabbit, or both;
S was a Squirrel, a Snark or a Sloth;
T was a Tiger, and terribly wroth;
U was a Unicorn truly unique;
V was a Vole, and a villain to squeak;
W, a Walrus, the Carpenter's chum,
Worshipping oysters but swallowing some;
X was Xanthippe; so Socrates thought;
Y was a Yak rather heavily fraught;
Z was a Zebra. No, begging your pardon,
Z was the whole Zoological Garden.

JINGLES.

There was an old man of Darjeeling
Who kept his eyes fixed on the ceiling;
    No wonder he missed
    Blue Peters at whist
And made such a bungle of dealing.

There was a young lady in Rome
Who couldn't keep quiet at home;
    A priest of St. Peter
    Once happened to meet her
And carried her up to the dome.

There were seven maiden ladies in Fakenham
Whose lovers, alas, had forsaken 'em;
    They sat by the fire
    Growing drier and drier
And wondered why no one had taken 'em.

There was a young lady in Cutch
Whose master was teaching her Dutch;
    Said he, "Pretty maiden,
    "I'll take you to Leyden."
Said she, "I was hoping as much."

N.B.—There was a Rao in Cutch after that.

There was a young lady in Shihuri
Who cut her aunt's throat in a fury;
   She was duly committed
   But promptly acquitted
On blowing a kiss to the Jury.

There was a young lady in Greece,
Whose conduct was all of a piece;
   Her parents both thought her
   A troublesome daughter,
And her aunt—an undutiful niece.

There was an old artist at Kew
Who ceased to discriminate hue;
   When the skies were all mellow
   With orange and yellow,
He cried, "What an exquisite blue!"

A lady who came to Calcutta
Was poisoned with clarified butter;
   "Oh Consomer jee,
   "You have killed me with ghee!"
The very last words she could utter,
     Or mutter,
That lady who came to Calcutta.

There was a young lady in Wales
Addicted to biting her nails;
  She was sent to Devizes
  To wait the Assizes
In one of Her Majesty's Jails.

QUESTION: CAN YOU RHYME *SAMPAN*?

A LITTLE girl lived near a tank
With a half-witted father, named Frank;
  They victualled a sampan
  With bread-pan, and jam-pan,
And sailed for nine years till she sank.

Translations from Horace and Martial.

K

HORAT., Lib. I, Carm. 38.

PERSICOS odi, puer, apparatus ;
Displicent nexæ philyard coronæ ;
Mitte sectari, roso quo locorum
    Sera moretur.

Simplici myrto nihil allabores
Sedulus cura : neque te ministrum
Dedecet myrtus, neque me sub arctâ
    Vite bibentem.

HORACE, Book I, Ode 38.

BRING me no Persian novelty, I beg, boy;
Twine me no linden coronet, and seek not
If in some nook now in the waning autumn
    Linger a rosebud;

Chiefly take heed thou never in adorning
Mar the plain myrtle; for it suits, the myrtle,
You the trim page, and me beneath the vine-bower
    Draining a wine-bowl.

HORAT., Lib. III, Carm. 9.

Hor.—

DONEC gratus eram tibi
    Nec quisquam potior brachia candidæ
Cervici juvenis dabat,
    Persarum vigui rege beatior.

Lyd.—

Donec non aliâ magis
    Arsisti, neque erat Lydia post Chloen,
Multi Lydia nominis
    Romanâ vigui clarior Iliâ.

Hor.—

Me nunc Thressa Chloe regit,
    Dulces docta modos et citharæ sciens,
Pro quâ non metuam mori
    Si parcent animæ fata superstiti.

Lyd.—

Me torret face mutuâ
    Thurini Calais filius Ornyti,
Pro quo bis patiar mori
    Si parcent puero fata superstiti.

Hor.—

Quid si prisca redit Venus
    Diductosque jugo cogit aeneo?
Si flava excutitur Chloe
    Rejectæque patet janua Lydiæ?

Lyd.—

Quamquam sidere pulchrior
    Ille est, tu levior cortice, et improbo
Iracundior Hadriâ,
    Tecum vivere amem, tecum obeam libens.

"OLD BROTH HEATED."

He—
    FAIR Nelly, when you loved me yet,
    And not another of our set
    Could coax you to caress him, ah !
    Your Will was happier than the Shah.

She—
    So, Willy, ere your fickle flame
    Burned incense to another's name,
    Your Nell was honoured in the town
    Beyond Queen Bess of high renown.

He—
    But now I've made a better choice,
    With such a touch and such a voice !
    And gladly would I seek the fray
    To fight and fall for Fanny Gray.

She—
    My passion now for Harry Lee
    Is only matched by his for me ;
    Twice would I perish in the strife.
    So Fate should spare my darling's life.

He—
    How would it do should Venus deign
    To yoke a parted pair again ?
    Old love is waking ; shall it wake
    And banish Fan for Nelly's sake ?

She—
    Though he is fair as stars above,
    And light as cork thy fickle love
    And crosser than the angry sea,
    With thee I'll live and die with thee !

MARTIAL.

I. 10.

PETIT Gemellus nuptias Maronillae
Et cupit et instat et precatur et donat.
Adeone pulchra est? immo foedius nil est.
Quid ergo in illâ petitur et placet? Tussit.

I. 89.

Garris in aurem semper omnibus, Cinna,
Garris et illud teste quod licet turbâ.
Rides in aurem, quereris, arguis, ploras,
Cantas in aurem, iudicas, taces, clamas,
Adeoque penitus sedit hic tibi morbus,
Ut saepe in aurem, Cinna, Caesarem laudes.

II. 20.

Carmina Paulus emit, recitat sua carmina Paulus.
Nam quod emas, possis iure vocare tuum.

MARTIAL'S EPIGRAMS.

I. 10.

GEMELLUS pays his fond addresses,
    Makes presents, pants, and prays, and presses.
So fair?—Nay, plain. The charms she offers
Lie in her cough and in her coffers.

I. 89.

Cinna, you whisper in one's ear,
And whisper each what all might hear.
In whispers laugh, and sing, and doubt,
And plead, and read your judgment out,
Complain, refrain, shed tears, and shout!
Till in your ailment's chronic phase
You whisper—even Cæsar's praise.

II. 20.

Rights pass by sale. From earliest times
    This doctrine has been known;
So Paullus buys his neighbour's rhymes
    And then recites his own.

(Another Rendering.)
"These lines are mine," sly Paullus cries;
And none can say that Paullus lies;
For Paullus owns what Paullus buys.

II. 35.

Cum sint crura tibi simulent quae cornua lunae,
  In rhytio poteras, Phoebe, lavare pedes.

II. 38.

Quid mihi reddat ager quaeris, Line, Nomentanus?
  Hoc mihi reddit ager: te, Line, non video.

II. 66.

Unus de toto peccaverat orbe comarum
  Anulus, incertâ non bene fixus acu.
Hoc facinus Lalage, speculo quo viderat, ulta est
  Et cecidit sectis icta Plecusa comis.
Desine iam, Lalage, tristes ornare capillos,
  Tangat et insanum nulla puella caput.
Hoc salamandra notet vel saeva novacula nudet,
  Ut digna speculo fiat imago tuo.

II. 71.

Candidius nihil est te, Caeciliane: notavi,
  Si quando ex nostris disticha pauca lego,
Protinus aut Marsi recitas aut scripta Catulli.
  Hoc mihi das, tanquam deteriora legas,
Ut collata magis placeant mea? Credimus istud:
  Malo tamen recites, Caeciliane, tua.

II. 35.

With limbs like crescent Luna's bandy
You'd find a horn a footbath handy.

II. 38.

What my Nomentan yield a-year is?
Well, rest from Linus and his queries.

II. 66.

O hasty blow! harsh mistress, hapless maid!
  One pin had slipped, one ringlet gone astray,
The glass avenged the failure it betrayed—
  Half shorn, half slain, poor stricken Barbara lay.
Deck, Lalage, nor thou thy guilty hair
  Nor maid that maniac head, in coming time;
But Salamander brand nor razor spare,
  So shall thy glass be sullied by its crime.

II. 71.

Most candid of critics, I note
  When I read you some couplets of mine,
Catullus or Marsus you quote
  To serve as a foil, I opine;
I value the courtesy shown
  But—wish you had read me your own.

II. 92.

Natorum mihi ius trium roganti
Musarum pretium dedit mearum
Solus qui poterat. Valebis, uxor.
Non debet domini perire munus.

III. 8.

Thaïda Quintus amat, quam Thaïda? Thaïda luscam.
    Unum oculum Thaïs non habet, ille duos.

III. 18.

Perfrixisse tuas questa est praefatio fauces.
    Cum te excusaris, Maxime, quid recitas?

III. 43.

Mentiris iuvenem tinctis, Laetine, capillis,
Tam subito corvus, qui modo cygnus eras.
Non omnes fallis; scit te Proserpina canum
Personam capiti detrahet illa tuo.

III. 46.

Exigis a nobis operam sine fine togatam.
    Non eo, libertum sed tibi mitto meum.
"Non est" inquis "idem." Multo plus esse probabo
    Vix ego lecticam subsequar, ille feret.
In turbam incideris, cuneos umbone repellet;
    Invalidum est nobis ingenuumque latus.
Quidlibet in causâ narraveris, ipse tacebo:
    At tibi tergeminum mugiet ille sophos.
Lis erit, ingenti faciet convitia voce:
    Esse pudor vetuit fortia verba mihi.
"Ergo nihil nobis" inquis "praestabis amicus?"
    Quidquid libertus, Candide, non poterit.

II. 92.

The honours of a sire of three
My epigrams have won for me;
So, Joan, we part; not one embrace;
'Twere ill to void our patron's grace!

III. 8.

"Thais is fair!" cries Quintus. "Who?"
"That lacks an eye." "Then he lacks two."

III. 18.

Your throat is sore, friend Maximus?
Then why not rest your throat—and us?

III. 43.

Your snowy locks, Lætinus, gone?
A raven, who wast erst a swan?
You, like your locks, will soon be lying,
For Death is near, and knows you're dyeing.

III. 46.

"What every day attend you? No;
Excuse me, but my man shall go.
Won't do? I'll prove it, he's the fitter;
I lag behind, he'll lift your litter.
His elbows cleave a charging crowd:
I'm far too slight, and far too proud,
I shall but hear you plead your cause,
While he will bellow fierce applause.
In rows he'll rail you loud and long;
Now, I 'refrain from language strong.'"
"What then? Shall friendship naught avail?"
"Yes, count on me———where he would fail."

III. 52.

Empta domus fuerat tibi, Tongiliane, ducenis:
　Abstulit hanc nimium casus in urbe frequens.
Collatum est deciens.　Rogo, non potes ipse videri
　Incendisse tuam, Tongiliane, domum?

III. 57.

Callidus imposuit nuper mihi copo Ravennae:
　Cum peterem mixtum, vendidit ille merum.

III 61.

Esse nihil dicis quidquid petis, improbe Cinna:
　Si nil, Cinna, petis, nil tibi, Cinna, nego.

III. 94.

Esse negas coctum leporem poscisque flagella.
　Mavis, Rufe, cocum scindere, quam leporem.

IV. 24.

Omnes quas habuit, Fabiane, Lycoris amicas
　Extulit: uxori fiat amica meae.

IV. 41.

Quid recitaturus circumdas vellera collo?
　Conveniunt nostris auribus ista magis.

III. 52.

Tongilian's mansion in the city
Was burnt to ashes! What a pity!
But thrice the price in presents came—
Now, did Tongilian light the flame?

III. 57.

(Adapted to the Simla water-famine.)

That Minx, my Simla landlord's daughter,
She sold me wine, and charged for water.

III. 61.

Each boon, you plead, is nothing, Cinna sly;
To you then, Cinna, nothing I deny.

III. 94.

" Dear friends, it's raw! my horsewhip! for I swear—"
" Ah! Brown, you'd carve your cook — to save your hare!"

IV. 24.

Lycoris all her lady friends inters.
Jove send my precious wife a friend of hers!

IV. 41.

Our poet in a comforter appears.
" Give *us* the worsted, Raucus, for our ears."

IV. 72.

Exigis, ut donem nostros tibi, Quinte, libellos.
  Non habeo, sed habet bibliopola Tryphon.
" Aes dabo pro nugis et emam tua carmina sanus?
  Non" inquis " faciam tam fatue."   Nec ego.

V. 9.

Languebam : sed tu comitatus protinus ad me
  Venisti centum, Symmache, discipulis.
Centum me tetigere manus aquilone gelatae :
  Non habui febrem, Symmache, nunc habeo.

V. 43.

Thais habet nigros, niveos Laecania dentes.
  Quae ratio est? Emptos haec habet, illa suos.

V. 47.

Nunquam se cenasse domi Philo iurat, et hoc est
  Non cenat, quotiens nemo vocavit eum.

VII. 98.

Omnia, Castor, emis : sic fiet, ut omnia vendas.

VIII. 10.

Emit lacernas millibus decem Bassus

Tyrias coloris optimi.   Lucrifecit.

" Adeo bene emit?" inquis.   Immo non solvet.

IV. 72.

My book ? oh, certainly. But stop.
I've sent them all to Tryphon's shop.
' What, cash for trash, sir, (you reply),
' I'm not a fool.'   No more am I !

V. 9.

You've cured my headache, Dr. Brown ;
Marched fifty gale-swept students down
Whose fifty-hands so chilled me, plague you,
What was a headache, is an ague !

V. 43.

Pyrrha has teeth whiter than snow ;
Thais's teeth are black as a crow ;
For Pyrrha's are bought, and Thais's grow.

V. 47.

" I rarely dine at home."   Poor sinner !
He's often there, but lacks the dinner.

(Idem Gallice redditum.)

" Jamais," jure Philon, " Je ne dine chez-moi."
Tu t'y trouves, Philon, mais tu n'as pas de quoi.

VII. 98.

There's Castor buying all creation :
He'll sell it soon——in liquidation.

VIII. 10.

" The purple cloak that Bassus wore
" Stood him in fifty pounds and more
" And cheap at that."   " How so," you say ;
" Why, Bassus never means to pay."

VIII. 12.

Uxorem quare locupletem ducere nolim,
  Quaeritis? Uxori nubere nolo meae.
Inferior matrona suo sit, Prisce, marito :
  Non aliter fiunt femina virque pares.

VIII. 13.

Morio dictus erat : viginti milibus emi.
  Redde mihi nummos, Gargiliane : sapit.

VIII. 43.

Effert uxores Fabius, Chrestilla maritos,
  Funereamque toris quassat uterque facem.
Victores committe, Venus; quos iste manebit
  Exitus, una duos ut Libitina ferat.

IX. 30.

Cappadocum saevis Antistius occidit oris
  Rusticus. O tristi crimine terra nocens!
Rettulit ossa sinu cari Nigrina mariti
  Et questa est longas non satis esse vias;
Cumque daret sanctam tumulis, quibus invidet, urnam
  Visa sibi est rapto bis viduata viro.

IX. 60.

Seu tu Paestanis genita es seu Tiburis arvis,
  Seu rubuit tellus Tuscula flore tuo;
Seu Praenestino te villica legit in horto,
  Seu modo Campani gloria ruris eras :
Pulchrior ut nostro videare corona Sabino,
  De Nomentano te putet esse meo.

VIII. 12.

"What, marry an heiress, and pocket my pride?
Why, she would be bridegroom and I should be bride!
Though mine be the wit and the rank and the riches,
Her chance is still even of wearing the breeches."

VIII. 13.

I bought a fool, and paid a hundred pound :
Disgorge, Gargilian, for his wits are sound !

VIII. 43.

Chrestilla and Fabius many a spouse have sped,
Waved funeral torches o'er each nuptial bed ;
Venus, mate both ! and seal their common doom—
One nuptial torch to light them to the tomb.

IX. 30.

Antistius fell on Cappadocia's shore :
   O guilty land ! O miserable crime !
Home next her heart his dust Nigrina bore,
   Blamed the swift barque, and all too fleeting time;
Envious his earth to Roman earth restored,
And mourned her love, twice widowed of her lord !

IX. 60.

Wreath, or of Pæstan or Tiburtine soil
   Or Tusculan the bloom and ruddy pride,
Or haply some Prænestine maiden's spoil,
   Or glory of Campania's country side,
Bid my Sabinus add a dearer charm
And deem thee of my own Nomentane farm.

L

IX. 98.

Vindemiarum non ubique proventus
Cessavit, Ovidi ; pluvia profuit grandis.
Centum Coranus amphoras aquae fecit.

XI. 96.

Marcia, non Rhenus, salit hic, Germane : quid obstas
    Et puerum prohibes divitis imbre lacus ?
Barbare, non debet submoto cive ministri
    Captivam victrix unda levare sitim.

XII. 23.

Dentibus atque comis, nec te pudet, uteris emptis.
    Quid facies oculo, Laelia ? non emitur.

XII. 25.

Cum rogo te nummos sine pignore, "non habeo," inquis.
    Idem, si pro me spondet agellus, habes.
Quod mihi non credis veteri, Telesine, sodali,
    Credis coliculis arboribusque meis.
Ecce, reum Carus te detulit : assit agellus.
    Exilio comitem quaeris? agellus eat.

XII. 89.

Quod lanâ caput alligas, Charine
Non aures tibi, sed dolent capilli.

IX. 98.

The vintage was not all in vain ;
Coranus found the downpour gain,
And bottled eighty quarts of—rain.

XI. 96.

Here Marcian jets not Rhenish play ;
German, dost drive that boy away ?
Quench, conquering wave, a captive thirst,
But Rome's young freeman claims thee first !

XII. 23.

Bold Lælia, locks and teeth you buy ;
You can't go shopping for an eye.

XII. 25.

" No cash to-day? That empty hand
   Holds plenty—if I pledge my land.
   What, doubt the oldest of your chums
   And trust my cabbages and plums ?
   Halt ! Carus quods you. Land defend you,
   And exile share, to cheer and tend you."

XII. 89.

Charinus wraps a muffler round his ears
To hide the hair-ache of advancing years.

THE ARTIST.

1.

O ARTIST, range not over wide,
   Lest what thou seek be haply hid
In bramble blossoms at thy side,
   Or shut within the daisy's lid.

2.

God's glory lies not out of reach.
   The moss we crush beneath our feet,
The pebbles on the wet sea-beach,
   Have solemn meanings strange and sweet.

3.

The peasant at his cottage door
   May teach thee more than Plato knew:
See that thou scorn him not: adore
   God in him, and thy nature too.

4.

Know well thy friends. The woodbine's breath
   The woolly tendril on the vine,
Are more to thee than Cato's death,
   Or Cicero's words to Catiline.

AD PICTOREM.

1.

PICTOR, materiem procul
  Arti parce tuæ quærere, ne rubi
Flos forsan teneat novus
  Aut claudat timidæ palpebra bellidis.

2.

Non te Numen in ardua
  Sectantem refugit. Quem pede conteris
Muscus, quot lavat Hadria
  Præsentem lapides dulce sonant Deum.

3.

Discas auspice rustico
  Quæ non olim acies illa Platonica
Cernebat. Fuge temnere
  Cui natura Dei contigit, et tua.

4.

Refert nosse tuos. Odor
  Ardet te clymeni, lanaque pampini :
Letum mitte Catonis, et
  Horrentem patriæ vulnera Tullium ;

5.

The wild rose is thy next in blood :
    Share Nature with her, and thy heart.
The kingcups are thy sisterhood :
    Consult them duly on thine art..

6.

Nor cross the sea for gems. Nor seek :
    Be sought. Fear not to dwell alone.
Possess thyself. Be proudly meek.
    See thou be worthy to be known.

7.

The Genius on thy daily ways
    Shall meet, and take thee by the hand ;
But serve him not as who obeys :
    He is thy slave if thou command.

8.

Be quiet. Take things as they come :
    Each hour will draw out some surprise.
With blessing let the days go home :
    Thou shalt have thanks from evening skies.

5.

Te vult, blanda soror, rosa :
  Pulcri quicquid erit hâc sociâ lege.
Te fratrem violæ petunt :
  Has et consilium posce, lucraberis.

6.

Gemmarum studio mare
  Nec transire decet : nec petere : at peti :
Te demissa superbia
  Solum sustineat. Siste potens tui :

7.

Sic dignam Genius lubens
  Erranti in triviis corripiet manum ;
Nec, si jusserit, obsequi
  Cura ; sed Genio fortiter impera.

8.

Æquâ mente vices lucro
  Appone : hora novum protrahet exitum.
Sanctos dege dies : tibi
  Sic grates tribuent alma crepuscula.

9.

Lean not on one mind constantly,
    Lest, where one stood before, two fall.
Something God hath to say to thee
    Worth hearing from the lips of all.

10.

All things are thine estate ; yet must
    Thou first display the title-deeds
And sue the world. Be strong ; and trust
    High instincts more than all the creeds.

11.

Assert thyself ; and by and by
    The world will come and lean on thee.
But seek not praise of men—thereby
    Shall false shows cheat thee. Boldly be

12.

Each man was worthy at the first,—
    God spake to us ere we were born ;
But we forget. The land is curst ;
    We plant the briar, reap the thorn.

9.

Audi quæ reserat Deus
  Haud uno ingenio fretus, at omnium ;
Est ut nisus in alterum
  Qui solus steterat concidat obruto.

10.

Orbem scis patrimonium :
  I, litem in populos infer, et occupa.
Virtutem colis insitam ?
  Fidat deterior relligionibus.

11.

Audax te tibi vindica :
  Mox fies columen civibus ; at fuge
Laudantem populum sequi
  Pomparum vacuâ captus imagine.

12.

Olim crevimus integri :
  Nos nondum genitos commonuit Deus.
At devotus ager gemit !
  At dumos serimus ! At metimus rubos !

The Artist.

13.

Remember, every soul He made
    Is different—has some deed to do,
Some work to work. Be undismay'd,
    Though thine be humble, do it too.

14.

Not all the wisdom of the schools
    Is wise for thee. Hast thou to speak?
No man hath spoken for thee. Rules
    Are well : but never fear to break.

15.

The scaffolding of other souls :
    It was not meant for thee to mount ;
Though it may serve thee.

Lord Lytton.

13.

Haud omnes animi pares :

   Haud debemus idem : pensa dedit Deus
Unicuique suum : tibi

   Si parvum dederit, perfice, perfice.

14.

Priscorum sapientia

   Non pro te sapiit.   Quidlibet eloqui
Debes ?   Non alius tibi

   Sermonem præiit.   Utere regulis ;

15.

Justum est scandere machinas

   Aptatas aliis mentibus ; at neque,
Si vis frangere, sit pudor ;

   Haud tali auxilio te decet evehi.

THE NIGHT IS STILL.

THE night is still, the moon looks kind :
    The dew hangs jewels in the heath :
An ivy climbs across thy blind,
    And throws a light and misty wreath.

The dew hangs jewels in the heath :
    Buds bloom for which the bee has pined :
I haste along, I quicker breathe :
    The night is still, the moon looks kind.

Buds bloom for which the bee has pined :
    The primrose slips its jealous sheath
As up the flower-watched path I wind
    And come thy window-ledge beneath.

The primrose slips its jealous sheath—
    Then open wide that churlish blind
And kiss me through the ivy wreath !
    The night is still, the moon looks kind.

Edith M. Thomas.

OMNIA VINCIT AMOR; QUIN TU QUOQUE CEDIS AMORI?

RURA silent, et Luna favens et amica tuetur;
 Ros humiles distinxit ericas:
Serta tuæ levia et nebulis incerta videri
 Tendit helix prope claustra fenestræ.

Rura silent, et ros humiles distinxit ericas:
 Floret ager, spes sera favorum;
Festinamus iter, levis exit anhelitus ore:
 Luna favens et amica tuetur.

Quâ mera mella, apibus dudum exspectata, patescunt,
 Quâ calicem nova primula fallit,
Custodita rosis quâ semita flectitur, adsum
 Cara, tuæ prope claustra fenestræ.

Tu, vigilem quoniam calicem matura fefellit
 Primula, tu mala claustra relaxa;
Hic inter teneras helices fac ut oscula libem!
 Luna favens et amica tuetur.

THE BELLMAN'S SPEECH.

"FRIENDS, Romans and countrymen lend me your ears!"
  (They were all of them fond of quotations)
So they drank to his health, and they gave him three cheers
  While he served out additional rations;

"We have sailed many weeks, we have sailed many days
  (Seven days to the week I allow,)
But a Snark upon which we might lovingly gaze
  We have never beheld until now!

We have sailed many months, we have sailed many weeks
  (Four weeks to the month you may mark)
But never as yet ('tis your Captain that speaks)
  Have we seen the least glimpse of a Snark.

Come hither, my men, while I tell you again
  The five unmistakeable marks
By which you may know, wherever you go,
  The warranted, genuine Snarks.

Let us take them in order. The first is the taste
  Which is meagre and hollow, though crisp;
Like a coat that is something too tight in the waist,
  With a flavour of Will-o'-the-Wisp.

TINNITORIS ORATIO.

"CIVES Romani" sic princeps incipit ore,
 Nec latuit nautas notior ille locus;
Immo tergeminâ propinant laude salutem
 Promenti duplices, vina cibumque, dapes;

"Multas hebdomadas, multosque per aequora soles
 (Septimus expletâ Sol ruit hebdomade)
Vela damus; studii solamen amabile nusquam
 Snarcharus attentos exhilaravit adhuc.

Multas hebdomadas, multosque per aequora menses
 (Quatuor hebdomadas, dicite, mensis habet)
Vela damus; dux ipse loquor; nec Snarcharus unus
 Dat quamvis subitâ cernere membra fugâ.

O comites, ne vos olim malus obruat error,
 Quæ prius edixi nunc iterare velim;
Sunt quibus egregiè generosi Snarcharus ortus
 Signatur, quovis sub Jove, quinque notæ.

Prima quidem—nam tanta ex ordine dicere fas est—
 Concavus et tenuis stet fragilisque sapor,
Qualis inest imo constrictæ pectore vesti,
 Te redolens, stagno fax generata gravi!

Its habit of getting up late, you'll agree
    It carries too far, when I say
That it frequently breakfasts at five o'clock tea
    And dines on the following day.

The third is its dulness in taking a jest ;
    If ever you venture on one
It groans like a creature surprised and distressed,
    And always looks grave at a pun.

The fourth is its fondness for bathing machines,
    Which it constantly carries about,
Believing they add to the beauty of scenes ;
    A sentiment open to doubt.

The fifth is ambition. It now will be right
    To describe you each separate batch,
Distinguishing those that have feathers and bite
    From those that have whiskers and scratch.

For, although common snarks do no manner of harm,
    Yet I feel it my duty to say
Some are Boojums "—The Bellman broke off in alarm,
    For the Baker had fainted away.

Idem Latine Versum.

Segnius in lucem somnos proflare diurnam
    Vos quoque fassuros credimus ore, boni,
Qui vespertinæ lentus jentacula mensæ
    Carpit, et in cœnam cras rediturus abit.

Ne forsan lateat nota tertia, discite, nautæ;
    Vix recipit crassâ Snarcharus aure sales;
Sed si forte comes quid luserit ore faceto
    Capta velut laqueo bellua, multa gemit.

Quarta satis constat; vaga tecta, natantibus apta,
    Quum juvat ire foras gestat ubique loci;
Scilicet his crescit species cultusque locorum;
    Haud equidem credo; sit sua cuique Venus.

Quinta, magistratus studium. Discrimina porro
    Proderit ancipitis commemorâsse necis;
Barbati lacerant infixis unguibus hostem,
    Plumigeri morsu viscera dilaniant.

Snarcharus est prædae; pugnabitis omine fausto;
    " Sed si Snarcharias Bujamis obveniat "—
Tinnitor pavet, et voces in faucibus hærent;
    Procubat exanimo corpore Pistor humi.

FROM "LYCIDAS."

ALAS! what boots it with incessant care
    To tend the homely slighted shepherd's trade,
And strictly meditate the thankless muse?
Were it not better done, as others use
To sport with Amaryllis in the shade
Or with the tangles of Neara's hair?

Milton.

FROM "THE PRINCESS."

FOR woman is not undevelopt man,
    But diverse: could we make her as the man,
Sweet Love were slain: his dearest bond is this,
Not like to like, but like in difference.
Yet in the long years liker must they grow;
The man be more of woman, she of man;
He gain in sweetness and in moral height,
Nor lose the wrestling thews that throw the world;
She mental breadth, nor fail in childward care,
Nor lose the childlike in the larger mind;
Till at the last she set herself to man,
Like perfect music unto noble words;
And so these twain, upon the skirts of Time,
Sit side by side, full-summed in all their powers,
Dispensing harvest, sowing the To-be,
Self-reverent each and reverencing each,
Distinct in individualities,
But like each other ev'n as those who love.
Then comes the statelier Eden back to men:
Then reign the world's great bridals, chaste and calm:
Then springs the crowning race of human kind.
May these things be!

Tennyson.

IDEM LATINE VERSUM.

HEU mihi! cur ovium custos inglorius erro,
    Quid tam perpetuo prodest renovata labore
Cura gregis? Quidve ingratam celebrasse Camœnam?
Ah, quanto melius patulæ sub tegmine fagi
Crinibus effusis vultum densare Neæræ
Aut timidam audaci tentare Amaryllida palmâ.

IDEM LATINE VERSUM.

GEMINA dissimile est natu, nec qualis origo
    Immatura viri; cujus si fiet ad instar
Prædulcem Veneris puerum mactaveris; ille
Conjugio nexisse solet meliore tenendos
Non simili similem, sed dissimilesque paresque.
His tamen in longis licet assimilarier annis;
Hic quiddam muliebre lucrabitur, illa virile;
Hic addet sibi suave decus, sine crimine mores,
Robora non ideo jacturus idonea pugnæ;
Illa simul, late sapiens, infessa fovebit
Prolem, et servabit mentem sibi prolis ad instar
Ingenuam et docilem; donec, quâ callidus arte
Carminibus didicit claris aptare poeta
Dulce melos, sic olim aptabitur illa marito.
Sic una tandem, propriis virtutibus etsi
Dissimiles similes ut quos concordia nexit,
Hic illi, illa viro venerabilis, et sine culpâ
Vivendi memores, sæclorum in fine sedebunt;
Connubioque novis completi viribus, ipsi
Ceu lætæ segetes, spargent et semina passim;
Sic genus humanum majorem scandere Olympum
Cernimus et castos resonare per orbem Hymenæos;
Unde siet proles, atavis generosior ætas;
Hæc felix faustusque Diespiter annuat ipse.

From the French of Victor Hugo.

FLOATS a sweet hymn where the aspens quiver,
   And the pilgrims of night hasten along;
Cheering the gloom of the dell by the river
      Sing, trembler, a song.

Sleep the worn crew on the verge of the eddy;
   Cease but the lava from vexing the deep,
Calm in its beauty it slumbers already;
      Sleep, weary one, sleep.

Is the day dark? Then we dream of gladness;
   Gleams on our tears a heavenly ray;
Cry we to God, who is near in sadness;
      Pray, sorrower, pray.

Life is our goal, and Death its portal;
   Doomed to the tomb is the whirl we cherish;
So that we merge in the Vast Immortal
      Let the perishing perish!

LA VIE.

LA vie est une fleur; l'amour en est le miel;
   C'est la colombe unie à l'aigle dans le ciel;
C'est la grace tremblante à la force appuyée,
C'est ta main dans ma main doucement oubliée.

LIFE.

LIFE is a blossom and its nectar—Love;
   A power to wed the eagle with the dove;
Bid timid grace on manly might recline,
And leave thy hand forgotten, dear, in mine.

Translations from the German.

SONGS OF A WANDERER.

I. Goodbye.

1.

GOODBYE, my love, for this
  Is the day we are to sever;
Give me a kiss—one kiss,
  For I leave thee now for ever!

2.

And a flower, a flower from the tree
  That is blooming by the wicket;
No fruit, no fruit for me,
  I shall not be here to pick it.

II. Afar.

1.

I will rest me here in the pleasant shade
  By the song of birds delighted;
Why is your song of my dearest maid?
What can ye know in this far-off glade,
  Of the happy love we plighted?

2.

I will rest me here by the brook so clear
  Where the sweetest flowers hang over;
Who can have sent you, flowrets, here?
Are ye a pledge from a maiden dear
  Sent to her absent lover?

III. A Morning Carol.

1.

FAINTLY breaks the day dawn pale;
  Deep in shadow lies the vale,
    Not a morn-bell ringing.

2.

Still and lone the greenwood seems;
Birds but twitter in their dreams,
  Not a songster singing.

3.

I have been a-field so long
I have conned this dainty song;
   I am up and singing!

IV. Lodging.

1.

A gentle kindly host was mine
   With whom I lately tarried;
A Golden Apple was his sign
   Upon a long bough carried.

2.

My host was the good apple-tree
   Where I took up my quarters;
Sweet was the meat he spread for me
   And fresh his sparkling waters.

3.

Right merry was his green hotel
   With many a light-winged guest,
They hopped about and feasted well
   Their glees were of the best.

4.

A grassy bed for sweet repose
   My kindly host he found me;
Himself he drew the curtains close
   Of cooling shade around me.

5.

I bad him reckon up the cost:
   He shook his head "Nay, never!"
My blessing on thee, kindly host,
   From root to crown for ever!

V. Home.

BREAK not, O bridge that dost tremble and sway;
   Crash not, O rock that dost frown on my way;
Sink not, O Earth; fall not, O Sky,
Ere we can meet, my love and I!

Uhland.

A HEAVY HEART.

WE are fading now, fair roses,
    That my love never wore;
Why did ye bloom, sweet roses,
    For a heart that is sore?

I muse and mourn, my angel,
    Those days at thy side;
Early, ere bud should open,
    To my garden I hied;

For my heart beat high at thy coming,
    My own, my sweet,
And all flowers, all fruit of my garden
    Were to cast at thy feet.

Now ye are fading, roses,
    That my love never wore;
Why did ye bloom, sweet roses,
    For a heart that is sore?

Goethe.

LORELEI.

I know not what omen is o'er me
   I feel so sad and low;
Or why it is before me,
   That tale of long ago.

The lift is cool and darkling
   And gently flows the Rhine;
But the mountain peak is sparkling
   In the gold of evenshine.

Above in her beauty beaming
   There sits a maiden fair;
Her jewels of gold are gleaming
   And she combs her golden hair;

Her comb itself is golden
   Her golden locks among;
And she sings a weird and olden
   And mighty Siren-song.

The boatman feels it move him
   To an ecstaty of woe;
He sees but the singer above him—
   Alas for the rocks below!

For the little bark will founder,
   And the boatman drown and die
For the glamour cast around her
   By the song of the Lorelei.

Heine.

A SONG OF LOVE.

LOVE on, while Love is near at hand;
    Love on, while Love is in thy keeping;
The hour is nigh when thou shalt stand,
    Among the graves, a-weeping!

See that the holy fire thou tend,
    Warm be thy heart, and frank thy greeting,
While in the bosom of thy friend
    For thee a warm, frank heart is beating.

To thee he lays that bosom bare;
    Each mood by kindly service gladden;
All hours to brighten be thy care,
    Nor one to sadden!

Nor let thy tongue be over-free:
    A word, if wrong, is lightly spoken;
"O God! I meant no ill" But he
    Is gone, heart-broken.

Love on, while Love is near at hand;
    Love on, while Love is in thy keeping;
The hour is nigh when thou shalt stand,
    Among the tombs, a-weeping.

Thou kneelest by his grave alone,
    Burying thy tearful eyes—alas,
No more to look into his own—
    Deep in the long damp grass,

And wailest: "Here upon thy grave
    Behold me weeping, waiting still;
Forgive me for the pain I gave;
    O God! I meant no ill!"

He sees nor hears thee ; nor his form
    Unto thy glad embrace is given ;
Nor lips whose kisses were so warm
    Can speak thee long forgiven.

He has forgiven thee long ; although
    On thee and on thy bitter jest,
Tears, burning tears would often flow—
    But hush ! He is at rest !

Love on, while love is near at hand ;
    Love on, while love is in thy keeping ;
The hour is nigh when thou shalt stand
    Among the graves, a-weeping.
Freiligrath.

THE FISHER MAIDEN.

COME, pretty fisher maiden,
    And steer your boat to land ;
Come, sit you down beside me,
    And listen, hand in hand.

So, lay your head on my bosom,
    And be not afraid of me ;
You are not afraid to venture
    Out on the stormy sea ?

My heart is like the sea, love
    With its storm, and ebb, and flow ;
And many a pearl for thee, love,
    Sleeps in the depth below.
Heine.

LA BELLE PÊCHEUSE.

VIENS donc, belle pêcheuse, et ramant à la rive
  Amarre ton canot ;
Apieds-toi pres de moi, que d'une âme pensive
  Je te soupire un mot.

Appuis-toi sur ce sein ; courage donc, courage ;
  L'esprit qui sans tremblant
Tous les jours se confie à la mer, à l'orage,
  Craindra-t-il son amant ?

Mon cœur est le miroir de la mer inquiète ;
  C'est vaste, c'est profond ;
La marée au-dessus, les vagues, la tempête,
  Et les perles au fond.

Heine.

THE TWO CHAMBERS.

THE heart has chambers twain :
  They shelter
Joy and her sister, Pain.

Here Joy her revel keeps :
  How nigh her
Pain, all a-weary, sleeps.

O Joy, for pity's sake
  Speak softly, softly,
Lest weary Pain awake.

Herm. Neumann.

SPRING SONG.

LIGHT and dear my heart can hear
  Sweetest bells a-pealing;
Little carol, far and near
  Trill the glad spring-feeling.

Trill and roam, and seek the home
  Where all flowers spring sweeter;
If thou seest a rose in bloom,
  Say I bad thee greet her.

Heine.

THE SILVER SEA.

A gleam upon the silver sea,
  A gleam of sunset only;
A little fishing-hut, and we
  Both mute and pale and lonely.

The clouds roll up, the billows rise,
  The sea-birds sail and hover;
The tears within thy lovesome eyes
  They gather and run over,

I saw, and on the yellow sand
  Beside thee kneeling lowly
Drank wildly from thy lily hand
  The drops I held so holy!

Those tears were poison! In their power
  One fierce regret I cherish
And day by day and hour
  I waste and pine and perish!

Heine.

SHELL SNAILS AND SNAIL SHELLS.

MISTRESS Snail her wit she shows;
She carries her house wherever she goes;
Wherein the wise see positive proof
That a Snail first taught us to build and roof.

So, if a good wife needs must roam,
She still in her heart should carry her home;
Nor leave it hung on a nail behind,
Out of sight and out of mind.

Nay, she better at home may bide
(Just as the man must tramp outside);
And as little dishonour shall thence derive
As the Queen-bee gets in the honey-bee's hive.

For the Queen-bee ever at home must stay,
Bidding her lieges fly away;
Also a fish, you understand,
Can never be easy long on land.

A snail must die, we know full well,
If a thief should carry away her shell;
And so, with the wife the world goes wrong
If you keep her away from her home too long.

Volkslied.

A WANDERER'S NIGHT-SONG.

THOU who of the Heavens art,
   Every ache and throe who stillest—
To the doubly stricken heart,
   Doubly free refreshing dealest—

I am weary! Let it cease:
   What are toil and joy and smart?
Sweetest Peace,
   Come, oh come upon my heart!

A FIGURE.

ON the mountains ever
   Is Rest.
Scarce an air a-quiver
Followest
In yonder pine.
The birds are all hushed in the forest;
   Wait, at thy sorest,
      And Rest in thine.

Goethe.

THE ROSE BUD IN THE HEATH.

FRESH and fair a rose bud grew,
   Rose bud in the heather;
Fair as dawn and fresh as dew!
Sprang the boy its grace to view,
   Charmèd altogether;
Rosy, rosy, rosy bud,
   Rose bud in the heather.

Cried the boy : " You shall be picked
   Rose bud in the heather ! "
Cried the rose : " You shall be pricked !
Thorns are sharp, and roses strict."
   Still the boy would gather
Rosy, rosy, rosy bud,
   Rose bud in the heather.

Naughty boy he dared to pluck
   Rose bud in the heather !
Rose bud stood on guard, and struck :
Boy must even bear his luck,
   Naughty boy to gather
Rosy, rosy, rosy bud,
   Rose bud in the heather.

Goethe.

A LITTLE SONG IN PRAISE OF WOMEN.

WOMEN are so named from winning;
    Man is but a sorry wight
Till a winsome woman woo him,
    Soul and body to delight.

Fitly mated, fairly fated—
    Miss a wife, and mar a life;
Torments vex who shun the sex,
    Dearth of joy, and dole of strife.

Charming, cheering—in her bearing
    Woman womanly is she—
Trusty, trustful, all endearing—
    Who so closely clings to me?

Rückert.

EVEN SONG.

EVEN is returning
   In her arms to fold
Earth for quiet yearning,
   Weary wood and wold.

Yet the brooklet gushes
   Headlong as before;
Past the rocks it rushes
   Onward ever more.

Knows no Vesper bringing
   Peace and solace nigh;
Hears no sweet bell ringing
   Tender lullaby.

Heart! that strivest ever,
   Craving rest denied,—
Ask of God the giver
   Peace at eventide.

Hoffmann von Fallersleben.

SLUMBER-SONG.

LIGHTLY, my little one, slumber a while;
Close the dear eyes that so lovingly smile;
Pillow thee warm on thy own mother's breast,
Rocked in my arms for thy cradle of rest!

Dreams of a joy in which earth has no part
Steal through the hush of thy innocent heart;
None but love's tears through the bright summer's day,
Freshen the roses that bloom on thy way.

Manhood is coming; when, worn with the fray,
Memory shall bear thee to childhood away;
Pleasure may woo, but woo thee in vain;
Oh! thou shalt long for thy cradle again.

Sleep, little angel, my angel of love!
Daylight is toying with starlight above;
Morning is here, and its herald be this—
Wake! for I seal thee my soul in a kiss!

Rückert.

SONG.

Of Thee! *(Von Dir.)*

THE stars they have voices the livelong night
For me, for me;
I know they are telling, O maiden bright,
Of thee, of thee.
They tell of the glance of thy starry eyes,—
How purer by far than the stars they shine;
So whisper the stars to me, to me,
The livelong night of thee.

The birds they are singing the whole day long
To me, to me;
I know that they carol in every song
Of thee, of thee.
They tell me thy voice has so pure a tone
That the nightingale listens and stills his own,—
So carol the birds to me, to me,
The whole day long of thee.

My heart it has ever a word to say
Of thee, of thee;
It names but thy name, be it night or day,
To me, to me.
It tells me its vow, it will ever adore,
And love thee for ever, and more and more;
And this is the tale my heart tells me,
At every beat, of thee!

Memories of the Nursery.

MEMORIES OF THE NURSERY.

If all the earth were apple-pie,
And all the seas were ink,
And all the trees were bread and cheese,
What should we do for drink?

  Daryá shor siyáhi ho,
  Zamín bákir khani,
  Sárá jangal dahi ho,
  To kaun dega páni?

Little boy blue, come blow up your horn,
The cows in the meadow, the sheep's in the corn;
But where is the boy that looks after the sheep?
He's under the haystack fast asleep!

Níl Baran Gareri dhol már terá,
Khet men pará sānr, jaūdád men pará bherá;
Kyá húá chhokrá jis ke zima'h bheri?
Pẽr talé suā hai Níl Baran Gareri!

Old mother Hubbard
Went to the cupboard
 To get her poor dog a bone;
When she got there,
The cupboard was bare,
 And so the poor dog got none!

  Dharmá Dái
  Hándi tak gayi
   Kutte ko dene hár;
  Wahán jab áyí
  To kuchh na páyí;
   Rah gayá rozahdár!

The man in the wilderness asked of me
"How many strawberries grow in the sea?"
I answered him, as I thought good,
"As many red herrings grow in the wood!"

"Rám Rám" bole jogi,
"Parbat men kitni machli hogi?"
Main ne kahā kih "Rám Rám
"Jitne talao men pholé ám!"

Humpty Dumpty sat on a wall,
Humpty Dumpty had a great fall.
Not all the Queen's horses, not all the King's men
Could put Humpty Dumpty together again.

Hamti Damti charhgayá chat;
Hamti Damti girgaya-phat,
Rájá ká paltān, Rani ke ghore
Hamti Damti kabhi na jore.

Little Bo-peep
Has lost her sheep,
And doesn't know where to find them;
Let 'em alone
And they'll come home
And bring their tails behind 'em!

Chhoti Momeri
Hargāyi bheri,
Kidhar se moh gayin gum;
Chhúti rahenge
To ghar men āwenge,
Wa sab ke pichhe dum!

Goosey, Goosey, Gander,
   Where shall I wander?
Upstairs, or downstairs,
   Or in my lady's chamber?
Old Daddy long-legs
   Would n't say his prayers ;
Take him by the left leg,
   And throw him downstairs!

Háns, Háns, Ráj Háns,
   Kidhar jane hotá ?
Upar jáwen, níche jáwen,
   Bibí-jí ka kotha ?
Budhā Behudā
   Chhor diyā namāz ;
Gor dharke phenk de,
   Pír pāē-darāz.

Dickory, dickory, dock ;
The mouse ran up the clock,
   The clock struck one,
   And down she run,
Dickory, dickory, dock.

Dekho re, dekho re, dekh !
Ghari bajegi ek !
   Jab ghantá huā,
   To kūd parâ chūhā,
Dekho re, dekho re, dekh !

Little Miss Muffet,
  Sat on a tuffet,
Eating of curds and whey,
  When a great ugly spider
  Came and sat down beside her,
And frightened Miss Muffet away.

   Mafiti Māi,
   Dalai malāi
     Ghās men baithke khāi,
   Jab bará sá makrá
   Uski sāri ko pakará,
     Bhāgē Mafiti Māi !

Jack and Jill went up the hill
  To fetch a pail of water,
Jack fell down, and broke his crown,
  And Jill came tumbling after.

Jak aur Jil pahár par charhé ;
Donow milke bālti bharé ;
Bālti bharke jab utare nīché,
To Jak girá āge aur Jil giri pichhé.

Higgledy piggledy, my fat hen !
She laid eggs for gentlemen,
Sometimes eight, and sometimes ten,
Higgleddy, piggledy, my fat hen !

Hakalī makalī, murghi merā !
Anda pārē bárah terah ;
Pār ke bhej de sāhib ká derah ;
Hakalī makalī murghi merā !

Memories of the Nursery.

" Lady Mary, quite contrary,
    How does your garden grow ? "
" Silver bells and cockle shells,
    And pretty maids all of a row."

" Miriam meri tirchhi terhi
    Phūtā gulistān ? "
" Chāndi ka ghanta wa kauri ka pāntā
    Wa larki khūb jawān ! "

" Pit-a-cake, pat-a-cake baker's man ! "
" So I will master, as fast as I can "
" Pit it and pat it, and mark it with ' C,'
And then it will do for Charlie and me ! "

" Dé nah chapatí, de, napaz ! "
" Phurti se denge bandah nawáz."
" Pito, wa páto, wa chháp de ' dāl,' "
" Kih sab koi jáne dukhi ká māl ? "

" Pussy cat, pussy cat, where have you been ? "
" I've been to London to look at the Queen."
" Pussy cat, pussy cat, what did you there ? "
" I frightened a little mouse under the chair ! "

" Phūs, phūs, kidhar se áyá ? "
" Rāni ka darshan shahar men paya."
" Phūs, phūs, udhar kya hūa ? "
" Kursi ke níche bhagá diya chūha ! "

Memories of the Nursery.

Simple Simon met a pieman
  Going to the fair;
Said Simple Simon to the pieman,
  " Let me taste your ware,"
Said the pieman to Simple Simon,
  " Let me see your penny ;"
Said Simple Simon to the pieman,
  " Why, I have n't any !"

Lāl Bujhakkar phire chakar ;
  Mēla jāē kalāl ;
" Babu," bole Lāl Bujhakkar,
  " Chakhen terā māl."
Itnā kahkar Lāl Bujhakkar
  Thām-le do phulauri ;
" Paisā dēnah, Lal Bujhakkar "
  " Atho phenk ke áyá kauri !"

Meeting by mistake
  Nothing could be fairer ;
This way ran the snake
  And that way ran the bearer.

Ghar ke sámhnē jhamp,
  Jhámp ke nichhe kankar ;
Udhar bhágé sámp
  Aur idhar bhágé Shankar !

GRAVIORA QUŒDAM.

LIBERTY.

(I owe the leading thought of these lines to the present Lord Bishop of Calcutta.)

Dash off the fetters! Let the slave be free!
   Freed be the Negro from the galling yoke ;
   Freed be the patriot from the tyrant's chain ;
Let thought and action, life and truth, be free.

   But see we err not, brother ; it were ill
To let the crystal chalice from thy hand
To shatter on the marble ; it were ill
If haply some adventurous charioteer
Should loose the unbroken colt upon the cliff
And rush with it to ruin.
                         But I have seen
A steed so noble that in full career
He sought, half knowing it, his rider's will ;
The light rein curving on the curvèd neck,
The varying accent of the kindly voice,
The very windings of the well-known way
Linked with a past obedience, were enough.
The gallant muscles strained in joyous play ;
The curb lay idle, and the steed was free !
   O Earth were Heaven, if only every soul
Should learn the perfect Liberty of Law ;
Burst the mean trammels of its lower self
And thus, exulting in the fullest play
Of its most God-like attributes and powers,
Should suffer God to lead it into joy !

SONNETS ON VEXED QUESTIONS.

I.

WILT thou believe ?   Let faith on reason rest :
But reason wisely ; t'were an idle hope
To mete an orbit with a microscope,
An angle with an acid.   For the test
Must ever vary with the varying quest.
Eye cannot image mind.   Enough to know
That God-like order in the realm below
Bespeaks a God ; to know that in man's breast,
There springs an eager longing to be blest.
Oh for a Christ to take us by the hand
And lead us, lift us to a better land !
   Hush, He is near, He calls thee.   For the rest
See that thy heart be pure, thy way be right,
Until the day-spring broaden into light.

II.

   He whose unerring instinct first descried
The veilèd attributes of finite space
Evolved alone his science, pace by pace ;
No facts collated, nothing verified
By slow observant watch.   But truth applied
Is other than truth abstract : and to trace
(As spirit read in a familiar face)
The record of the rainbow : to decide
From dark and lucid, narrow bars and wide,
The secrets of its solar starting place—
This is a power the giants of our race
   Have won in slowly toiling side by side.
Shall we be fools, my friends and stand aloof
Till Euclid set his seal on Frauenhofer's proof ?

III.

And if we leave the circle and the square
And matter of the spheres, and higher soar
Himself, the all-Creator, to explore
And man, his mystic image and his heir,
Seek we new methods.   Let the Spirit bear
Joint witness with our spirits.   Be the lore
Writ for all time by holy men of yore
Our list, our handbook ; till, as we compare
Things spiritual—lo! an order fair
Where all seemed chaos ; and the bars before
Deemed (for we missed the message that they bore)
   A blemish on the rainbow, shall declare
More truth, more beauty than its brightest dye
Sends to the heaven-set arch athwart the Western sky !

IV.

"Your God of love created to betray,
"And nerved us but to suffer."   Brother, no ;
For is not sin the protoplasm of woe ?
Shall fire not burn ? Shall sword forget to slay ?
For that He knew the peril of the way
And willed to save His children from the throe,
The ripened fruit of error—bad them know
Joy pure and perfect, therefore did He say
"Thou shalt not." So that haply, day by day,
Taught of the edged steel, the fire aglow,
From sharper dangers and a fiercer foe
   They walk unscathed, who loving Him obey.
Walk in His law, and thou shalt find it so,
And know a Father's hand in all His work below.

V.

Spencer, methinks the man who thinks the most
May think to poorest purpose, so you trace
Some self-sown seed of worship in our race,
Some pale, thin image of a comrade lost
Or foe, though slain, still hated, till a host
Of little men-made gods, more frail and base
Than they who made them, crowd and darken space.
Thou flower of Evolution! Thine the boast
To give mankind a devil's Pentecost
And read religion backwards! Thine the grace
Six thousand years of progress to efface
And chill our garnered sunshine into frost.
Take back thy boon, O thou who thinkest most,
Nor rend away our God, to offer us a ghost.

www.ingramcontent.com/pod-product-compliance
Lightning Source LLC
Chambersburg PA
CBHW031829230426
43669CB00009B/1278